Leader's / Catechist's Manual

Catholicism and Society

Rev. Edward J. Hayes
Rev. Msgr. Paul J. Hayes
and James J. Drummey

C.R. Publications
345 Prospect Street
Norwood, Massachusetts 02062

© 1997 C.R. Publications
ALL RIGHTS RESERVED

NIHIL OBSTAT
Msgr. William E. Maguire
Censor Librorum

IMPRIMATUR
Most Rev. John C. Reiss
Bishop of Trenton
December 20, 1996

The Nihil Obstat and Imprimatur are official declarations that a book or pamphlet is free of doctrinal or moral error. No implication is contained therein that those who have granted the Nihil Obstat or Imprimatur agree with the contents, opinions, or statements expressed.

Cover design by Jeff Giniewicz
Printed in the United States of America
ISBN 0-9649087-6-X

Contents

How to Get the Most Out of This Book 5
1. The Christian Call to Holiness 13
2. Every Life Is a Vocation 18
3. The Future of Christian Marriage 24
4. Between Husband and Wife 31
5. Between Parent and Child 36
6. The Teenage Years 41
7. Between Family and Society 45
8. Between Family and God 55
9. The Modern Woman 58
10. The Senior Citizen 62
11. The Eighth Person 65
12. Christian Stewardship 71
13. Morality in Public Life 76
14. Cults and the New Age Movement 80
15. Advocates of Atheism 85
16. A Movement That Changed the World 89
17. Marxism and Religion 93
18. The Christian Response 98
19. You Can Make a Difference 101

How to Get the Most Out of This Book

The purpose of *Catholicism and Society* is to take the basic moral principles given to us by our Blessed Lord in the Sermon on the Mount and apply them to the fundamental problems facing the family and society today. Because it spells out the duties and responsibilities of Catholic lay people in the modern world, *Catholicism and Society* will appeal to a wide audience—from high school students to senior citizens. It is an excellent text for adults, whether in formal courses, informal study groups, or marriage preparation programs; for college and university students; and for those in Catholic high schools or parish religious education programs.

The book is a valuable tool because it offers not only a full-year study of applied Christianity, but it can also be broken down into mini-courses. Some examples:

1. A course on marriage and family life (chapters 3-8).

2. A course on life issues—contraception, abortion, and euthanasia (chapter 7).

3. A course on some of the major social problems of the day (chapters 9-14).

4. A course on the atheist-communist impact on our way of life in the twentieth century (chapters 15-18).

There are other possibilities and variations as well, depending on what you want to offer or what religious voids need to be filled. Many parishes are scheduling adult education programs during the year and offering courses one night a week for five or six weeks. A series of this type can be very successful, especially during Advent or Lent, and this volume, or its companion texts, *Catholicism and Reason* and *Catholicism and Life*, would be very appropriate for such a series.

But whatever material and format you choose, few books lend themselves better to discussion than *Catholicism and Society*. The text will give Catholics the ammunition they need to do battle with those who are challenging and violating basic human and Christian values. Armed with this information, the Catholic laity will then be able, in the words of Pope John Paul II, "to act with the serene conviction that grace is more powerful than sin because of the victory of Christ's cross."

Specific suggestions for stimulating interest and initiating discussion can be found under the individual chapters. These suggestions, of course, are not all-encompassing, but they should provide some practical ideas for the catechist or group leader. The chapters contain more than enough information for classes of forty-five to ninety minutes, but they need not be confined to one class; in some cases, this will not be possible because there is such a great amount of material to be covered.

It will be up to the individual catechist to decide how much time should be spent on each chapter and how the time should be divided between lecture and discussion. Some groups are more responsive than others and make the teacher's job easier. Whatever the situation, no catechist should have difficulty preparing an interesting and effective class.

Generally speaking, the suggestions for presenting the material will be helpful whether you are teaching high schoolers or adults, although there are certain topics, questions, and projects that will be more appropriate for one age group than another. The catechist will have to be the judge of that.

In addition to the specific tips on teaching from *Catholicism and Society*, the following general comments, not necessarily in the order of their importance, may be helpful.

1. *Read the entire book and catechist's manual before you begin teaching.* Not only should you do this to familiarize yourself with the entire course, but it will be useful if you are questioned about a matter that will be covered later in the course. You could then answer the question briefly, note that it will be taken up in more detail at another time, and refer the questioner to the appropriate chapter for additional information.

2. *State your goals at the beginning of each class.* Tell the

students what you expect to cover and what is expected of them. Be yourself, be in charge, keep things simple and concrete (it is not easy to grasp abstract concepts), give clear directions, and have a sense of humor. Use your lesson plan as a road map with different routes. Don't be afraid to switch directions and even to take up something new to keep the attention of the class. Start out with some life experience that is familiar to the students, then present the doctrine or message you want to convey in that particular class, and finally attempt to elicit some faith response from them.

Try to vary your lessons with different methods and activities. Use some lecture, some dialogue, some student presentations, some problem-solving, some projects, and even some games (adapt "Wheel of Fortune" or "Jeopardy" or "Family Feud" or "Hangman" to the information to be covered). Ask the students to rate things in the order of their importance (the Beatitudes, vocations, the qualities of a good husband or wife, reasons for joining a cult, etc.) to stimulate discussion. Ask them their top five choices of teen problems.

3. *Although the material in* Catholicism and Society *can be presented effectively in lecture form, the ideal way to develop it is through discussion.* Students are more likely to remember things if they have had a chance to talk about them, ask questions, and even figure out some of the answers themselves. By discussion, it should be made clear, we do not mean an aimless stream of consciousness where everybody's opinion is equally valid and where nothing is resolved. We mean rather an atmosphere where the teacher teaches and the student learns; where questions, comments, and dialogue are encouraged under the guidance and direction of the catechist; where facts are stated by the catechist if the students do not come up with them; and where the catechist summarizes the matter discussed at the end of the class, answering all questions as well as possible and trying to resolve all doubts.

4. *Instead of merely stating the points to be covered, catechists should seek to draw the information out of the students.* Catechists should be constantly asking questions, making the students think, and inviting them to participate in the class.

When you first ask a question, do not direct it to a particular student lest the others in the class assume that they are safe and can stop paying attention. Ask the question first of the entire class and then, if no one volunteers an answer, direct it to a particular person. Do not allow a few students to monopolize the discussion. Try to involve everyone, especially those who seem not to be paying attention. Be careful not to embarrass the shy or reticent student, but try to bring him or her out of their shell. When students ask what you think about some matter, turn the question back to them and ask, "What do you think?" Your goal is to keep all the students involved.

5. *Keep the class interesting and current through the use of stories, anecdotes, and up-to-date items related to the subject matter.* Storytelling is an effective way to make a point, as our Lord proved with his use of parables. Have the students bring into class pertinent items from newspapers and magazines, especially those critical of the Church, so you can correct the misinformation. Get them in the habit of watching for these things and you will have a successful class. Remember, however, that media accounts of religious issues are often slanted, out of context, misleading, or just plain wrong. Insist that authentic documents, not some reporter's biased view of a Church teaching, be used to form the basis of any valid discussion.

6. *Define all terms, even if it seems unnecessary.* You should not assume that any religious term is understood correctly, so ask the students what it means and then spell out the definition for them. Unless the students understand exactly what you are talking about, you will either lose them or misinform them. A Catholic dictionary or encyclopedia, or the glossary section of the *Catholic Almanac*, will be most helpful in providing definitions. A good secular dictionary, even though not Catholic, can also provide accurate definitions of religious terms.

And don't be afraid to have the students memorize some of these definitions. As Pope John Paul said, "A certain memorization of the words of Jesus, of important Bible passages, of the Ten Commandments, of the formulas of profession of the faith, of the liturgical texts, of the essential prayers, of key doctrinal ideas, etc., far from being opposed to the dignity of young Christians, or constituting an obstacle to personal dialogue with the Lord, is a real need. . . . We must be realists. The blossoms, if we may call them that, of faith and piety do not grow in the desert places of a memory-less catechesis" (*On Catechesis in Our Time*, n. 55).

7. *Use the chalkboard and other visual aids as much as possible.* The old saying that one picture is worth a thousand words is still true. Children remember about 10 percent of what they hear, 50 percent of what they see and hear, and 90 percent of what they see, hear, and do. You can talk about abortion and its horrors for hours and not convince anyone that it is evil, but one video showing the beautiful developing child at 12 weeks, or the crushed and bloody remains of an aborted baby, can make a profound impression.

Not all issues can be as graphically portrayed as abortion, but any maps, videos, slides, pictures, etc., that can be used to illustrate a point will add immeasurably to your class. Simply writing things on the board will also make a difference in getting the material across to the students. Or holding up flash cards that say AGREE or DISAGREE after you make a statement. Do not neglect any tool that will make your class more informative and interesting.

8. *Review what you have covered previously.* It is a good idea to use the beginning of each class to summarize, or have the students summarize, what has been covered thus far, particularly in the previous class. In this way, you will know what is getting across and what needs to be repeated. If time permits, you could give brief quizzes at the beginning of class to prepare the ground for the next phase of the course. Quizzes and tests are important, even in once-a-week religion classes, if we expect the students to take the subject seriously.

9. *State the position of the Church clearly and unequivocally.* This is most important since many Catholics are confused today on where their Church stands. Your job is not to give your own opinion or that of some popular theologian, but

rather the definitive teaching of the infallible Church of Christ. "Catechists for their part," Pope John Paul said, "must have the wisdom to pick from the field of theological research those points that can provide light for their own reflection and their teaching, drawing, like the theologians, from the true sources, in the light of the magisterium. They must refuse to trouble the minds of the children and young people, at this stage of their catechesis, with outlandish theories, useless questions, and unproductive discussions, things that St. Paul often condemned in his pastoral letters" (*On Catechesis in Our Time*, n. 61).

This adherence to the truth is a solemn responsibility. Make sure that the class always knows what the Church's teaching is and the reason for that teaching. If you do not know the answer to a question, do not try to fool the students. Tell them that you will find the answer—and then do so. Do not get bogged down in certain areas, and do not worry if you cannot completely convince all your students about the merits of a specific teaching. Do your best to present the view of the Church and then leave it to the Holy Spirit to enlighten the minds of your listeners.

10. *Assign projects and homework so as to involve the class more deeply in the course.* This course offers a good opportunity to encourage familiarity with the Holy Scriptures, and teachers ought to assign readings in the Bible. Every student ought to spend some time reading and reflecting on the Sermon on the Mount. There are also numerous reference works that the students should be assigned to consult and report on to the class. Have one or two students give a five-minute talk each class. This will prepare them to talk about Christ and the teachings of his Church just as freely and intelligently as they talk about sports or movies or music.

Speaking of references, there are certain books that are invaluable to catechists and should be a part of their own library. These books include a Bible, a Catholic dictionary, a one-volume Catholic encyclopedia, a Catholic almanac, the *Catechism of the Catholic Church*, a history of the Catholic Church, a life of Christ, a dictionary of the saints, a good question-and-answer book like *Catholic Replies*, and, for this volume, such pertinent papal documents as Pope John Paul's *Letter to Families* and his *Gospel of Life*. The teacher should also read some good Catholic periodicals to keep up with what is happening in the Church.

11. *Encourage daily prayer, frequent reception of the Sacraments, and the performance of good works.* Take advantage of the numerous reminders throughout the course to mention the necessity of daily prayer, at least weekly Mass and Communion, and frequent Confession. Urge the students to carry out works of charity, either individually or collectively. Begin and end each class with a prayer, inviting the students to suggest prayers and to lead the class in saying them. A decade of the rosary is a good way to start a class period. The teacher can be an actual grace for the students by inspiring them to do good and avoid evil and always to remain close to Jesus and his Church. Catechists who demonstrate a sincere interest in the well-being of their students, who pray with them and for them, who are available to them after class for any help or advice they may need can have a positive and long-lasting influence on the young people entrusted to them.

Effective catechesis depends upon "the faith, hope, and love of catechists, responding to God's grace by growing in these virtues and ministering to others," said the Bishops of the United States in *Sharing the Light of Faith*. "The person of the catechist is the medium in which the message of the Faith is incarnated. Whether catechists be parents, teachers, religious, priests, bishops, or any other of God's people, their witness to faith plays a pivotal role in catechesis."

12. *For high school religion teachers, acquaint the parents of your students with the course.* There are three things necessary for a successful CCD or religious education program—good books, good teachers, and interested parents. We have provided the first requirement and contributed to the second. The third is up to you. Contact all the parents at the beginning of the year, invite them to a meeting to explain the course to them, urge them to send their children to class faithfully, and invite them to visit the classroom or to contact you if they have any questions or suggestions. Some students will tell

parents that they don't want to go to class because "we're not learning anything." Parents who know what is being taught to their children will not be swayed by that argument.

13. *It is important for the catechist to realize that the work of helping others to grow and mature in the Christian life is primarily the work of the Holy Spirit.* The catechist, Pope John Paul said, "must be very much aware of acting as a living, pliant instrument of the Holy Spirit. To invoke this Spirit constantly, to be in communion with him, to endeavor to know his authentic inspirations must be the attitude of the teaching Church and of every catechist" (*On Catechesis in Our Time*, n. 72)

"The fundamental tasks of catechists," the Bishops of the United States said in *Sharing the Light of Faith*, "are to proclaim Christ's message, to participate in efforts to develop community, to lead people to worship and prayer, and to motivate them to serve others" (n. 213). In order to be effective teachers, the Bishops said, catechists "must have a solid grasp of Catholic doctrine and worship, familiarity with Scripture, communications skills, the ability to use various methodologies, understanding of how people grow and mature, and of how persons of different ages and circumstances learn" (n. 211).

But perhaps most important, the Bishops said, "the catechist must be fully committed to Jesus Christ. Faith must be shared with conviction, joy, love, enthusiasm, and hope. . . . To give witness to the gospel, the catechist must establish a living, ever-deepening relationship with the Lord. He or she must be a person of prayer, one who frequently reflects on the Scriptures and whose Christlike living testifies to deep faith. Only men and women of faith can share faith with others, preparing the setting within which people can respond in faith to God's grace" (n. 207).

Chapter 1

The Christian Call to Holiness

Purpose: The purpose of this chapter is to spell out the obligation of a Christian to seek the reform of modern society through application of the Beatitudes and the other principles enunciated by Christ in the Sermon on the Mount.

Tips for Teachers: The first part of this class will necessarily have to be taken up with seating arrangements, attendance, and rules for classroom conduct. It will be important for the catechist of high school students to state clearly what is expected of the teenagers. The atmosphere created in the first class can set the tone for the year. Catechists should express their policies and expectations clearly and firmly so as to prevent misunderstandings and problems from arising later on.

One obvious and essential rule is that only one person speaks at a time, either the catechist or one of the students who has been properly recognized. A courteous and respectful atmosphere is the only setting in which religion or any other subject can be effectively presented by the catechist and completely understood by the students.

The catechist should also mention such things as homework assignments, quizzes, tests, and special projects—in other words, the various techniques and methods that will be used to develop the subject matter, impart knowledge to the students, and encourage them to practice their Faith.

Once the preliminaries are over, the remainder of the class should be spent discussing the general nature and purpose of the course, with emphasis on some of the more interesting and challenging subjects to be covered—vocations; marriage and divorce; husband-wife, parent-child relationships; the teenager and dating, drinking, drugs, and driving; contraception, abortion, and euthanasia; the modern woman; the senior citizen; racial justice; morality in public life; cults and the New Age; and the Christian response to atheism and Marxism-Leninism.

The catechist can then get into the material in chapter 1. There are a lot of points to be covered and the questions that follow will be helpful in highlighting the most important areas. Some time ought to be spent discussing the Sermon on the Mount and the Beatitudes, and how the students can put these principles to work in their own lives. General discussion of these principles is not enough; the students must come up with specific and concrete ways of letting their light shine in the world, of performing good works (e.g., corporal and spiritual works of mercy) that might otherwise be left undone.

Several approaches could be used to convey a correct understanding of the Beatitudes. For example, the catechist could ask the students to write a story illustrating one of the Beatitudes. Or a matching test could be given in which the Beatitudes are listed in the left-hand column and a description of each, in scrambled order, is given in the right-hand column:

A. Blest are the poor in spirit	Those who show compassion and forgiveness to others
B. Blest too ... the sorrowing	Those who direct all their activities to the service of God and neighbor
C. Blest are the lowly	Those who carry out the will of God despite ridicule, harassment and bodily harm
D. Blest are those who hunger and thirst for holiness	Those who remain loyal to Christ no matter what suffering confronts them
E. Blest are they who show mercy	Those who patiently prevent strife and promote harmony wherever they go
F. Blest ... the singlehearted	Those who are not concerned about material things
G. Blest ... the peacemakers	Those who are submissive to God and docile to his will
H. Blest are those persecuted for holiness' sake	Those who strive for interior goodness and live hand in hand with God

(The answers are E, F, H, B, G, A, C, D.)

Another point that ought to be emphasized is the obligation of the Christian to speak out regardless of the consequences. It will take courage to stand against the tide of public opinion and suggest Christian solutions to the social problems of the day, but this is what it means to be a Christian, a follower of Christ. It will be difficult to act as Christ wants us to act, but our reward in heaven will be great.

Topics for Discussion:

1. What is the Christian call to holiness?
2. What are some of the good things that people leave undone?
3. What can you do to restore all things in Christ? To let your light shine before the world?
4. What did Vatican II mean when it said that a member of the Church "who fails to make his proper contribution to the development of the Church must be said to be useful neither to the Church nor to himself"?
5. Why must followers of Jesus expect ridicule and persecution?
6. Explain the following: "What man thinks important, God holds in contempt."

Some Questions and Answers:

1. What are the corporal and spiritual works of mercy?
A. The chief corporal works of mercy are: to feed the hungry, give drink to the thirsty, clothe the naked, visit the imprisoned, shelter the homeless, visit the sick, and bury the dead.

The chief spiritual works of mercy are: to instruct the ignorant, counsel the doubtful, admonish the sinner, comfort the sorrowful, bear wrongs patiently, forgive all injuries, and pray for the living and the dead.

2. "Why should I have to tell people about doing the right thing?" a friend asks. "That's the priest's job." How would you answer?
A. If there is one thing the Second Vatican Council made clear, it was the obligation of the laity to spread the teach-

ings of Christ in society. Lay people have access to places where priests and religious men and women cannot go. The office, the factory, the construction site, the classroom, the store, the neighborhood gathering—these are all places where the clergy has little or no influence or opportunity to preach the Gospel.

But an informed and committed lay person, who knows what Christ expects of him or her, can do a lot of good in these circumstances. And people who would turn a deaf ear to the clergy might be more receptive to the same message when it comes from a fellow worker, fellow student, or neighbor. How many chances have you passed up to let the light of Christ shine before friends and acquaintances?

Projects:

1. Make a new person feel comfortable at your work, school, or social gathering.
2. Perform a corporal or spiritual work of mercy every day.
3. Write a short story illustrating how one of the Beatitudes can be lived out today.
4. List ten of the spiritual and moral principles mentioned in the Sermon on the Mount.
5. Bring in to class five newspaper or magazine advertisements stressing the pursuit of material goods and pleasures.
6. Read Vatican II's *Decree on the Apostolate of the Laity*, or one of Pope John Paul's encyclicals listed below, and summarize its major points.

References:

Angelica, Mother. *Mother Angelica's Answers, Not Promises*
Catechism of the Catholic Church
Catholic Almanac
Catholic Encyclopedia. Edited by Fr. Peter M.J. Stravinskas
Drummey, James J. *Catholic Replies*
Flannery, Austin, O.P. *Vatican Council II: The Conciliar and Post Conciliar Documents*
Grisez, Germain. *Christian Moral Principles*
_____. *Living a Christian Life*
Hardon, John A., S.J. *The Catholic Catechism*
_____. *Modern Catholic Dictionary*

_____. *The Question and Answer Catholic Catechism*
John Paul II, Pope. *Christifideles Laici* ("The Lay Members of Christ's Faithful People")
_____. *Crossing the Threshold of Hope*
_____. *Evangelium Vitae* ("The Gospel of Life")
_____. *Redemptoris Missio* ("The Mission of the Redeemer")
_____. *Sollicitudo Rei Socialis* ("On Social Concern")
_____. *Veritatis Splendor* ("The Splendor of Truth")
U.S. Catholic Conference. *Basic Teachings for Catholic Religious Education*
_____. *Sharing the Light of Faith: National Catechetical Directory for Catholics of the United States*
Wuerl, Donald, Lawler, Thomas and Lawler, Ronald. *The Catholic Catechism*
_____. *The Teaching of Christ*

Chapter 2

Every Life Is a Vocation

Purpose: The purpose of this chapter is to show the careful consideration that must be given to the choice of a state in life since it involves both our happiness in this life and in the next life.

Tips for Teachers: The first step might be to ask the students what vocation or occupation they have chosen or think they might choose. Then point out how important our choice of a vocation is and how closely connected it will be with our eternal salvation. Note that there are only four states in life in which we can serve God and explain the nature of each. By way of demonstrating the importance of all four vocations, have the students write a 300-word defense of the vocation they most desire, and then a 300-word defense of the vocation that least appeals to them.

When discussing the religious life and the factors that must be considered before deciding to become a priest, brother, or sister, encourage young people to think about a religious vocation and to pray for God's guidance in that choice. Invite a person who has chosen the religious life to speak to the class on the reasons for his or her choice, or send the students out to interview a priest, brother, or sister.

This is one of the few times that young people will have an opportunity to discuss religious vocations; do not fail to take advantage of this chance to plant a seed that might flower into a religious vocation in a few years. The question will inevitably arise about those men and women who have left religious life or who have been involved in scandalous actions. Point out that the religious life should be judged by the actions of those priests, brothers, and sisters who have remained holy and who have continued their dedicated and unselfish service to God and his people. Just as a college should not be judged by the students who drop out, so the religious life should not be judged by those who leave.

Since most teenagers will choose married life as their vocation, it is imperative that they understand the reasons why marriages fail so that they can avoid the same pitfalls. Point out the qualities that must be found—and those that must be avoided—in a prospective spouse. Ask the students to list five qualities that they would most like to find in a spouse, and five qualities that they would least like to find. Urge them to be very realistic in the choice of a marriage partner because the choice is for life.

Also emphasize the necessity of agreement before marriage on such matters as the purpose of marriage, the number of children and their upbringing, religious practice, standard of living and finances, in-laws, outside activities, and so forth. A strong religious faith is essential and will help couples to get over some of the rough spots.

Many people today are very critical of the Catholic Church for not permitting couples in troubled marriages to get a divorce. The solution to troubled marriages, in most cases, is not easier divorce, but more careful preparation for marriage. The advice offered in this chapter, if understood and accepted by young people, could save them a lot of heartaches in the future. Make sure they get the message.

Topics for Discussion:

1. What are the four states in life in which we can serve God? Which is the most important?

2. Which state have you chosen or do you intend to choose?

3. What are the four requirements for religious life? Which is the most important and why? Would you add any others?

4. Have you ever thought you might have a religious vocation? Have you done anything about it?

5. Why is the priest another Christ?

6. What are some of the reasons for unsuccessful marriages?

7. What are some of the areas in which engaged couples should reach agreement?

Some Questions and Answers:

1. Should anyone look down on the vocation of another person?

A. Certainly not. Every person, no matter their state in life or occupation, is working toward the same goal: happiness here and hereafter. Each one of us is called by God to serve him in some way in this life. If we carry out the mission God has given to us, he will reward us in heaven. The respect that is due to everyone's vocation was well expressed by Oliver Nelson when he said, "If all the garbage men and all the preachers quit at the same time, which would you miss first?"

2. A friend says, "There must be something wrong with that man across the street. He never got married." How would you respond?

A. There is no law that says everyone must get married. There are many people who have conscientiously chosen the single state and are very happy in it. Having no family responsibilities, single people often devote their lives to serving God and others. There are some who even consecrate their virginity or celibacy to God. Their spiritual contribution is highly regarded by the Church and these single people should be the objects of our praise, not our ridicule.

3. What can be done to encourage religious vocations?

A. Young people are just as idealistic today as they ever were. All they need to be guided into the priesthood or the religious life is information, formation, and inspiration. The ultimate source of vocations is the family. The real vocation directors are Catholic mothers and fathers. How many parents ask their children if they have considered a religious vocation? How many families pray for vocations? How many parents spend as much time encouraging religious vocations as they do pushing their children into a wide variety of school and outside activities? If parents, priests and sisters, and religion teachers will inform children about the joys of religious life, form them through prayer and encouragement, and inspire them through good example to serve God in this special way, young people will respond to God's call and vocations will be plentiful again.

4. Why doesn't the Church change its position on celibacy and let priests get married? Other churches have

married clergy. That would mean a lot of vocations to the priesthood.

A. If you look at churches that allow married priests, you will find that their vocations are not increasing. So letting priests marry is not the answer to the clergy shortage. Priestly celibacy, which Pope Paul VI called "a brilliant jewel," has been practiced in the Catholic Church since the fourth century for a number of reasons.

First, it follows the example of Christ himself, who promised great rewards to those who have "given up home, brothers or sisters, father or mother, wife or children or property for my sake" (Matthew 19:29). Second, it allows priests to focus exclusively on serving Christ and the Church, without at the same time worrying about wives and children. They are called to a higher fatherhood and have many more "spiritual children" than in an ordinary family. Married clergy in other religions, torn between their family and their congregation, have expressed appreciation for the celibacy required of Catholic priests.

Third, celibacy provides space and time for serious prayer and development of a deep bond with Christ, whom the priest is called to share with the world. Fourth, it is a foreshadowing of heaven where there will be no marriage. And fifth, it is a wonderful example of commitment and sacrifice under difficult circumstances; it gives credibility to priests who ask their people also to make great sacrifices for God.

It is important to remember that no one is required to become a priest; that celibacy is not forced on priests but is freely chosen by them after years of training, reflection, and prayer; that celibacy is no more responsible for unfaithful priests than marriage is responsible for unfaithful husbands and wives; and that a great number of priests, religious, and laity all over the world are today living inspiring lives of voluntary and consecrated celibacy.

5. Ralph says, "My girlfriend and I are smart. We're living together now to see if we're suited for each other. When we get married, we'll be ready for marriage." What would you say?

A. Ralph and his girl are kidding themselves. Apart from the immorality of the situation, and the deliberate defiance of God's divine plan, their arrangement is not very practical. Sooner or later, Ralph and his girl will run into a problem. If it is a particularly difficult one, all they have to do to get away from the problem is to terminate their arrangement. They have no lasting or solid commitment to each other and they know that they can get out of a troublesome situation very easily, so they have little incentive to try to solve a difficult problem. Their arrangement is the very opposite of true love, which always involves putting one's partner first.

The most happily married couples have to face problems and work them out with love and patience and understanding. It is the spirit of unselfishness that makes marriages work, but the unselfishness must exist before the marriage if it is to flourish during married life. It is a fact that the divorce rate among couples who lived together before marriage is just as high as among couples who did not. So there is no evidence to indicate that living together before marriage will ensure a happy and trouble-free married life.

Projects:

1. Write a 300-word paper on the vocation you find most appealing.

2. Write a 300-word paper on the vocation you find least appealing.

3. Interview a priest, brother, or sister and ask them why they chose a religious vocation and whether their expectations have been fulfilled.

4. Write an article about the most unforgettable priest, brother, or sister you have known.

5. List five qualities that you would most like to find in a prospective husband or wife.

6. List five qualities that you would least like to find in a prospective husband or wife.

References:

Bonacci, Mary Beth. *Real Love Answers Your Questions on Dating, Marriage, and the Real Meaning of Sex*

Burke, Cormac. *Covenanted Happiness*

Catechism of the Catholic Church

Cochini, Christian, S.J. *Apostolic Origins of Priestly Celibacy*

Drummey, James J. *Catholic Replies*

Fox, Fr. Robert J., and Mangan, Fr. Charles. *Until Death Do Us Part*

John Paul II, Pope. *Letter to Families*

_____. *Familiaris Consortio* ("The Role of the Christian Family in the Modern World")

Kippley, John F. *Marriage Is for Keeps*

Marks, Frederick W. *A Catholic Handbook for Engaged and Newly Married Couples*

Paul VI, Pope. *Populorum Progressio* ("On the Development of Peoples")

Sacred Congregation for the Clergy. *Only for Love: Reflections on Priestly Celibacy*

Vatican II. *Decree on the Appropriate Renewal of the Religious Life*

_____. *Decree on the Ministry and Life of Priests*

_____. *Decree on Priestly Formation*

_____. *Dogmatic Constitution on the Church*

Chapter 3

The Future of Christian Marriage

Purpose: The purpose of this chapter is to provide a clear understanding of the divine origin and purpose of Christian marriage, and to show the practical wisdom of the Church's teaching on divorce

Tips for Teachers: One way to get into this chapter would be to review the problems facing Christian marriage today, including the widespread attacks on marriage and the family. The next step is to set forth the teaching of the Catholic Church on marriage as expressed in the documents listed below. Have the students read and discuss these documents, as well as the scriptural passages from Genesis, the Gospels, and the letters of St. Paul.

Emphasize the importance of the sacrament of Matrimony as a source of God's grace. This supernatural assistance is the only thing that will give married couples the strength to overcome the difficulties and disappointments that arise from time to time. It would seem that many married couples have forgotten that they have this special sacrament, so make sure that the students know it.

The section on the twofold purpose of marriage is probably one of the most important parts of this book. A lot of marital problems could be eliminated if spouses had a proper understanding of the true philosophy of Christian marriage. The catechist must explain the life-giving and love-giving aspects of marriage and stress that disregard for either aspect violates both the nature of man and woman and the plan of God. The two aspects are inseparable and one cannot be used to the exclusion of the other.

As noted in the text, the correct philosophy of marriage can be expressed by a triangle. Have the students make posters illustrating this point. Another way of gaining insight into Christian marriage would be to invite a Catholic married couple to talk to the class about what marriage and matrimony mean to them. Needless to say, the catechist had better make sure that the invited couple is in agreement with the Church's teaching on marriage and responsible parenthood.

Having spelled out the Christian philosophy of marriage, the catechist can then take up the difficult and even tragic issue of divorce. You might discuss the reasons usually given to justify divorce, whether they have any merit, and whether many of these problem areas could have been avoided with proper instruction and preparation before marriage. Or whether they could be solved even now with professional counseling and an unselfish and loving effort by the quarreling spouses. With so many divorces in the United States each year, and the havoc this has caused in our society, the wisdom of our Lord's teaching becomes more obvious every day.

A point that must be made in connection with this topic is that we should not judge or condemn people who are divorced, not only because it would be wrong to do so but also because there will be children in the classroom whose parents are divorced. This is a sensitive subject and, while the teaching of Jesus and his Church must be presented and explained, it should be done with charity. Remind the students that divorce does not separate a Catholic from the sacraments, but only remarriage while one's partner is still alive, since this constitutes adultery.

Questions about mixed marriages, impediments to marriage, the reasons for declaring certain marriages null and void will be asked. Information and guidelines about these matters can be obtained from your parish priest, your diocesan chancery or marriage tribunal, or the family life bureau in your diocese.

Conclude the chapter on a note of optimism by acknowledging that while Christian marriage is confronted with serious difficulties today, the situation is not hopeless. The institution will survive and flourish if couples respond to the Christian call to holiness and spread by word and example the true philosophy of Christian marriage.

Topics for Discussion:

1. What are some of the problems facing the Christian family today?

2. What is the twofold purpose of marriage?
3. What are some of the reasons why couples seek a divorce?
4. What can be done to promote and defend Christian marriage?
5. What is the difference between marriage and matrimony?

Some Questions and Answers:

1. Why do marriage and the family offer the only real hope for the future of society?
A. The family is the foundation of society. It is in the family that children learn to get along with one another, to assume certain responsibilities and obligations, and to prepare for the day when they will become parents and conscientious citizens themselves. The importance of a loving, stable, Christian environment for the education and training of children cannot be emphasized too much. The only place where such an environment can be found is in the family circle. It is this kind of atmosphere that will produce the responsible, unselfish, and dedicated leaders that are so necessary if we are to Christianize the society in which we live.

2. What themes run through the Church's major statements on marriage?
A. The themes stressed by the shepherds of Christ's Church over the past seven decades are that marriage was instituted by the Creator at the beginning of the human race; that Jesus later raised marriage to a sacrament which gives married couples the supernatural grace they need to live according to the divine plan and to attain their eternal salvation; and that the Christian family is the foundation of society and a manifestation to all the world of the union that exists between Christ and his Church.

3. How does the love between husband and wife symbolize the love between Christ and his Church?
A. St. Paul tells us that the passage in Genesis about a man leaving his mother and father and clinging to his wife so that the two become one is "a great foreshadowing" of Christ

leaving his Father in heaven and clinging to his bride, the Church, so that the two become one. St. Paul also sees the unselfish love of a husband and wife, a love that inspires spouses to make great sacrifices for each other, as symbolic of the love of Christ for the Church, a love so great that Christ laid down his life for the Church.

4. Maureen says, "I know of a married couple who really hate each other. The Church should let them get divorced and not force them to live together." How would you reply?

A. First of all, the Church cannot change its teaching on divorce because divorce was prohibited by our Lord himself. Christ, looking down through the centuries, could see the chaos that easy divorce would bring to marriage and the family, so he refused to allow it. Second, while the situation cited by Maureen is undoubtedly true in some cases, the small percentage of such hostile relationships cannot justify removing the Church's ban on divorce. The vast majority of divorces, like the vast majority of abortions, are sought by people looking for a convenient way out of a situation they themselves created. Third, the Church does not force any couple to live together. If a marital arrangement becomes intolerable, the Church will permit a separation but not a divorce or remarriage. Fourth, there are Church agencies and concerned Catholics who can help the victims of a broken marriage.

5. How do you answer people who say an annulment is a "Catholic divorce"?

A. An annulment or, more properly, a decree of nullity, is a declaration by the Church, through a diocesan agency known as a tribunal, that what appeared to be a valid marriage was defective in some way at the time that the couple exchanged their vows. It is not the dissolution of a valid marriage, but rather a decree that a valid marriage never existed. And by the way, it does not make illegitimate any children of that union.

The usual reasons for granting an annulment in the past were fraud, force, or fear. It had to be proven that at least one of the parties was not free to marry, lacked the physical ability and mental competence to fulfill the duties and responsibilities of the married state, or was forced into the union by parental or societal pressure.

The reasons were expanded somewhat when the revised Code of Canon Law was published in 1983. Canon 1095 says that persons incapable of contracting a valid marriage would include those "who lack the sufficient use of reason; who suffer from grave lack of discretion of judgment concerning essential matrimonial rights and duties which are to be mutually given and accepted; who are not capable of assuming the essential obligations of matrimony due to causes of a psychic nature."

The last phrase—"causes of a psychic nature"—has generated much controversy in recent years as the number of annulments granted has skyrocketed. Those favoring more annulments have said that not enough attention was paid in the past to psychological causes, while those favoring fewer annulments have argued that too much weight is being given to psychological grounds today.

The solution lies somewhere in between the two positions, according to Pope John Paul II, who said that marriage tribunal judges must always "guard against the risk of misplaced compassion, which would degenerate into sentimentality." He said that while the Church recognized "the great difficulties facing persons and families involved in unhappy conjugal living situations," it could not declare valid marriages null and void "without doing violence to the truth and undermining thereby the only solid foundation which can support personal, marital, and social life."

6. Why doesn't the Church approve homosexual relationships if they involve two people who love each other?

A. Homosexual behavior has always been condemned by the Church because it is contrary to the divine plan and violates the life-giving aspect of the sexual relationship. The Bible is quite clear on the evil of homosexual behavior, and the prohibitions enunciated in Scripture are just as applicable in contemporary society as they were thousands of years ago. For instance, the Lord said to Moses, "If a man lies with a male as with a woman, both of them shall be put to death for their abominable deed" (Leviticus 20-13). And St. Paul said, "God therefore delivered them up to disgraceful passions. Their women exchanged natural intercourse for unnatural, and the men gave up natural intercourse with women and burned with lust for one another. Men did shameful things with men, and thus received in their own persons the penalty for their perversity" (Romans 1:26-27).

Bear in mind, however, the distinction the Church makes between homosexual orientation, which is not sinful provided there is no genital relationship with a person of the same sex, and homosexual acts, which "are intrinsically disordered and may never be approved in any way whatever" (Sacred Congregation for the Doctrine of the Faith, *Declaration on Certain Problems of Sexual Ethics*, n. 8).

Projects:

1. Write a paper on one of the references cited below.
2. Make a poster showing the triangle philosophy of marriage.
3. Clip five stories from newspapers or magazines showing a false picture of marriage.
4. Invite a married couple to talk to the class.
5. Invite a priest to demonstrate the marriage ceremony, with members of the class taking the places of the wedding party.

References:

Bonacci, Mary Beth. *Real Love Answers Your Questions on Dating, Marriage, and the Real Meaning of Sex*

Burke, Cormac. *Covenanted Happiness*

Catechism of the Catholic Church

Dannemeyer, William. *Shadow in the Land: Homosexuality in America*

Dilenno, Joseph A., M.D., and Smith, Herbert F., S.J. *Homosexuality: The Questions*

Drummey, James J. *Catholic Replies*

Fox, Fr. Robert J., and Mangan, Fr. Charles. *Until Death Do Us Part*

Harvey, John F., O.S.F.S. *The Homosexual: New Thinking in Pastoral Care*
_____. *The Truth About Homosexuality*
John Paul II, Pope. *Evangelium Vitae* ("The Gospel of Life")
_____. *Familiaris Consortio* ("The Role of the Christian Family in the Modern World")
_____. *Letter to Families*
_____. *Veritatis Splendor* ("The Splendor of Truth")
Kippley, John F. *Marriage Is for Keeps*
Lawler, Ronald, Boyle, Joseph, and May, William E. *Catholic Sexual Ethics*
Marks, Frederick W. *A Catholic Handbook for Engaged and Newly Married Couples*
Paul VI, Pope. *Humanae Vitae* ("On Human Life")
Pius XI, Pope. *Casti Connubii* ("On Christian Marriage")
Pontifical Council for the Family. *The Truth and Meaning of Human Sexuality*
Pornography's Victims. Edited by Phyllis Schlafly
Sacred Congregation for the Doctrine of the Faith. *Declaration on Certain Problems of Sexual Ethics*
_____. *Letter to the Bishops of the Catholic Church on the Pastoral Care of Homosexual Persons*
Vatican II. Pastoral *Constitution on the Church in the Modern World*

Chapter 4

Between Husband and Wife

Purpose: The purpose of this chapter is to discuss the basic principles and qualities that are necessary for a happy marital relationship between a husband and wife and that will help them to overcome difficulties and disappointments.

Tips for Teachers: Begin by pointing out that any successful marriage must rest on the three pillars of information, communication, and application. Then discuss each of these pillars individually, emphasizing the importance of sound information and effective communication. You can show how communication can break down by giving a short message to one student and then having it whispered to each student in class, one by one. When the exercise is complete, there may not be much resemblance between your original message and the last student's version of it. Spend some time on the true definition of communication and the basic principles that will ensure genuine communication between husband and wife and also, you might add, between parents and children. Consistent application of these principles will contribute greatly to a harmonious home situation.

The next step is to discuss thoroughly five of the basic qualities that can lead to a happy marriage. The students may think of other qualities, but these five are certainly important. Make sure that you convey the proper Christian attitude toward chastity and sexual love in marriage. Misinformation abounds in these areas and this might be the only time that some of the students will hear the correct viewpoint. Be very frank and truthful with them, and you might help them to avoid problems later in life. The qualities of unselfishness and affection can be illustrated by having the class put the theme of the O. Henry story in a different context, and by having them suggest five ways that married couples can show their affection for each other.

Discuss the differences between men and women regarding their respective vocations and their intellectual and emotional characteristics. And give St. Paul fair treatment by reading what he said about husbands and wives and explaining exactly what he meant.

The section on the crosses in marriage must also be honestly and frankly presented. These crosses affect many marriages, and candidates for marriage must be prepared to shoulder them and to unite them with the sufferings of Christ on the cross. The answer to the trials in marriage is not to run to the divorce court at the first sign of trouble, but to bear the crosses patiently and courageously as the spouses promised to do on their wedding day.

Finally, note that marriage is a one hundred percent proposition for both parties. The real test of a good marriage is when each partner gives the other credit for contributing the most to the marriage. A happy marriage will not eliminate all of life's problems, but it will make it easier to cope with them.

Topics for Discussion:

1. What are the basic foundations on which marriage rests?

2. What are some of the important qualities of a good marriage? Which is the most important?

3. Do you think that the old instruction before marriage that is quoted on pages 46-47 of the text should be included in the current marriage ceremony?

4. Can the answers to a happy marriage be found in best-selling sex manuals?

5. What are some of the intellectual and emotional differences between men and women?

6. Is marriage a fifty-fifty proposition?

7. Explain the meaning of the statement, "Success in marriage means not only finding the right mate, but also being the right mate."

Some Questions and Answers:

1. Why is constructive and open communication so important in marriage?

A. Surveys have indicated, and marriage counselors have agreed, that most of the problems that weaken and destroy marriages can be traced to poor communication between spouses. They are not open and honest with each other; they are often more interested in expressing their own opinion than in listening to what their partner has to say; they are unable to discuss their disagreements calmly and lovingly. Conversely, those couples who unselfishly put their spouse's feelings ahead of their own, who are willing to give a little for the good of the marriage, who treat their partners as they would like to be treated—these people experience peaceful and happy marriages.

It is only common sense that couples who can freely talk about not only the big decisions in their lives, but also the petty grievances and irritations, and do so in a patient and constructive way, will have little or no trouble getting over the rough spots in marriage that trip up stubborn, selfish, and cold-hearted spouses.

2. Fred asks, "Are you really serious when you say that chastity in marriage is both possible and desirable? Husbands and wives aren't made of stone, you know."

A. Yes, we know that married couples are not made of stone, but we really are serious. We know that spouses have to abstain from sexual relations at certain times—before and after the birth of a child, during unavoidable separations, for reasons of health, and so forth—and that unselfish couples who want to live according to the Creator's divine plan can and do practice continence during these times without any traumatic effects.

This being so, we believe that couples who wish to space out births for serious reasons do not automatically have to resort to artificial methods of contraception. With mutual love and support for each other, couples can practice the virtue of chastity. We are not saying that it is easy, but with constant prayer and frequent recourse to the sacraments, Catholic husbands and wives with strong convictions about life and love can enjoy a happy and holy married life. And these periods of abstinence can enhance marital relations by elevating them from purely mechanical actions to deeply spiritual unions.

The time has come for those who call themselves followers of Christ to raise their sights and aim for Christian ideals. We have been wallowing in pagan mediocrity for too long.

3. Can you give some examples of affection in marriage?

A. Just for openers: telling your spouse often how much he or she is loved and appreciated; taking the children out so he can work on a project; bringing her flowers for no special reason; preparing him a candlelight supper with his favorite menu; being hospitable to his or her family and friends; treating her extra special when she is pregnant; being a good mother or father to the children; going away together for some time alone; making a married couples retreat or a marriage encounter.

4. Susan says that St. Paul was nothing but a first-century male chauvinist with all his talk about wives being inferior to their husbands. Comment.

A. St. Paul never said that wives were inferior to their husbands. His words have been taken way out of context. What he did say was that wives should submit to their husbands "as the church submits to Christ." And that husbands should love their wives "as Christ loved the church." Since Christ gave up his life for the Church, what greater tribute could Paul pay to wives than to ask husbands to be willing to imitate Christ? What more profound analogy could the Apostle draw than to compare Christian marriage with Christ's intimate union with his Church? If wives serve their husbands in the same spirit that the Church serves Christ, and husbands care for their wives with the same devotion that our Lord has for the Church, what better arrangement could any spouse ask for?

Projects:

1. Do a report on one of the references listed below.
2. Interview a happily married couple to find out the reasons for their successful marriage.
3. Take the basic theme of the O. Henry story and present it in different circumstances, either in writing or by acting it out.
4. Have two students play the role of spouses trying to work out a problem.

References:

Bonacci, Mary Beth. *Real Love Answers Your Questions on Dating, Marriage, and the Real Meaning of Sex*
Burke, Cormac. *Covenanted Happiness*
Catechism of the Catholic Church
Dannemeyer, William. *Shadow in the Land: Homosexuality in America*
Dilenno, Joseph A., M.D., and Smith, Herbert F., S.J. *Homosexuality: The Questions*
Drummey, James J. *Catholic Replies*
Fox, Fr. Robert J., and Mangan, Fr. Charles. *Until Death Do Us Part*
Harvey, John F., O.S.F.S. *The Homosexual: New Thinking in Pastoral Care*
_____. *The Truth About Homosexuality*
John Paul II, Pope. *Evangelium Vitae* ("The Gospel of Life")
_____. *Familiaris Consortio* ("The Role of the Christian Family in the Modern World")
_____. *Letter to Families*
Kippley, John F. *Marriage Is for Keeps*
_____. *Sex and the Marriage Covenant*
_____. and Kippley, Sheila. *The Art of Natural Family Planning*
Lawler, Ronald, Boyle, Joseph, and May, William E. *Catholic Sexual Ethics*
Marks, Frederick W. *A Catholic Handbook for Engaged and Newly Married Couples*
Paul VI, Pope. *Humanae Vitae* ("On Human Life")
Pius XI, Pope. *Casti Connubii* ("On Christian Marriage")
Pontifical Council for the Family. *The Truth and Meaning of Human Sexuality*
Vatican II. Pastoral *Constitution on the Church in the Modern World*

Chapter 5

Between Parent and Child

Purpose: The purpose of this chapter is to discuss the purpose of the family, the role of each member of the family, and some practical guidelines for raising and training children.

Tips for Teachers: Begin by reviewing the serious problems that face Christian families today and the necessity for cooperation between parents and children to overcome them. Explain the purpose of the vocation of marriage and the solemn responsibility parents have in working with God to bring a new life into the world and then to educate and train that child. The Christian family is a team and everyone has a specific role to play and certain duties and obligations to fulfill. Outline those roles and duties and discuss how each member can contribute to a happy home. Pope John XXIII's statement on this matter should also be discussed.

The education and training of children is a huge task for parents. The task is made easier, however, by the fact that the home is a natural place for education. Mention the importance of beginning the training of children in both religious and secular matters as early as possible. Most children are pretty well formed by the time they go to school, so the preschool years must not be neglected.

During these years, children are eager to learn and their minds are like sponges. It is a great opportunity to tell them about God and the Church, Mary and saints, and Christian values. They should not be allowed to watch too much television, but should be encouraged to read and to play nicely with their brothers and sisters and friends. If open and honest communication between parents and children is developed and encouraged in these early years, it will help to prevent communications problems later on, particularly in the teenage years.

The matter of discipline—what it is, why it is necessary, and how it can be beneficial both to parents and children—should be taken up next. Point out that effective discipline must be fair, firm, consistent, constructive, and balanced with love. Seek examples to illustrate these points. Ask the students what disciplinary rules they would draw up if they were parents.

The area of sex education is very controversial and confused today. That positive and prudent instruction should be given to children is undeniable, but the best way to go about this is widely debated. Discuss some of the principles suggested in this chapter and recommend the references below for more detailed advice and answers to some of the typical questions about sexuality that are often asked.

One point that ought to be stressed is modesty in dress. This will be a hard issue to deal with because of the extremes to which modern fashions have gone, but it should not be skipped over. Catholic young people must set a high standard of morality, but how can they do so unless they are encouraged by parents and teachers of religion classes?

Lastly, it should be noted that parenthood is not easy; it requires prayer, hard work, sacrifice, patience, perseverance, and love. Urge the students to cooperate with their parents in every way they can so as not to make a difficult job more difficult. A harmonious Catholic home is attainable today if all members of the family do their share and work for the good of the family.

Topics for Discussion:

1. How important is proper home training in raising children?

2. What is meant by the statement, "Parents must be acknowledged as the first and foremost educators of their children"?

3. Should parents monitor their childrens' reading material and television viewing?

4. Should parents check on who their childrens' companions are?

5. True or false: Spare the rod and spoil the child.

6. Where, when, and by whom should sex education be given to children?

7. How many children do you plan to have if you get married?

Some Questions and Answers:

1. What is the purpose of the family?
A. The purpose of the family is to educate and train children to know, love, and serve God in this world so as to be happy with him in the next life.

2. How can parents communicate love to their children?
A. Parents can show love and affection for their children by giving them understanding and support, by offering them advice and encouragement in whatever worthwhile things they do, by showing an interest in what they are saying, by always being available to them, by answering their questions honestly and fully, by praising them and complimenting them, and by telling them straight out and frequently that they are loved and wanted and appreciated. Parents can do a lot for a child's sense of worth and self-esteem through words and actions that communicate love and affection.

3. How can children express their love and thanks to their parents?
A. Children can show their parents how much they are loved and appreciated by telling them so, by showing them respect and obedience, by asking their advice, by discussing things with them, and by always being open and honest with them. Children should fulfill their duties as members of a family and should do so automatically instead of forcing Mom or Dad to nag them or to threaten some punishment. The "Golden Rule" is still the best advice: Treat other people as you would want them to treat you.

4. How important is religious training and example in the home?
A. It is absolutely vital to the spiritual growth and well-being of a child. No parochial school or CCD program, no matter how good it is, can make up for a lack of religious training at home. Unless religious instruction in the classroom is supplemented and reinforced at home, and vice-versa, a vital part of a child's training will be neglected. Family prayer, Bible reading,

religious discussion, and frequent reception of the sacraments as a family are indispensable aids in the molding of Catholic youth.

5. Why is modesty in dress so important?
A. The human body was created by God and, therefore, it is gòod. It is to be used, however, as God intended. The physical attraction between males and females is perfectly natural and was designed by the Creator to lead them into marriage and into sexual activities which are both life-giving and love-giving. Sexual intimacies outside of marriage are immoral and sinful, and followers of Christ are to avoid immodest thoughts, words, actions, or dress that could lead to illicit sexual pleasure. Chastity outside of marriage can be compared to a castle, with modesty being the moat that surrounds and protects the castle. Once the moat has been crossed, the castle is in trouble. Once modesty has been disregarded, then chastity is endangered.

Modesty is very much ignored today—on television, in newspapers and magazines, and in the revealing clothes that people wear. Those who dress immodestly can be an occasion of sin for others who may be sexually aroused by the skimpy outfits and bathing suits they see. Those who advertise their wares so blatantly should not be surprised if someone expects them to make available the product they have been advertising. One doesn't have to dress in Victorian styles to be modest, but one should try to wear decent clothes and bathing suits.

Projects:

1. Do a report on one of the references listed below.
2. List five ways that you could improve the atmosphere in your home—and then do them.
3. Voluntarily perform an extra chore around the house.
4. Draw up a list of disciplinary rules that you think would be fair to children.
5. Bring any problems or questions you have to your parents first.
6. Act out a solution to a problem, first from the parents' side and then from the childrens' viewpoint.

References:

Bonacci, Mary Beth. *Real Love Answers Your Questions on Dating, Marriage, and the Real Meaning of Sex*

Catechism of the Catholic Church

Drummey, James J. *Catholic Replies*

Fox, Fr. Robert J. *The Gift of Sexuality: A Guide for Young People*

John Paul II, Pope. *Familiaris Consortio* ("The Role of the Christian Family in the Modern World")

_____. *Letter to Families*

John XXIII, Pope. *Ad Petri Cathedram* ("Near the Chair of Peter")

Kuharski, Mary Ann. *Raising Catholic Children*

Pontifical Council for the Family. *The Truth and Meaning of Human Sexuality*

Pulling, Pat. *The Devil's Web*

Sattler, Vern. *Challenging Children to Chastity*

U.S. Catholic Conference. *Basic Teachings for Catholic Religious Education*

Vatican II. *Declaration on Christian Education*

_____. *Pastoral Constitution on the Church in the Modern World*

Chapter 6

The Teenage Years

Purpose: The purpose of this chapter is to explain the concept of authority and to discuss the problem areas of dating, drinking, drugs, and driving.

Tips for Teachers: Begin by writing the words "generation gap" on the board and initiating a discussion on what it means, whether there is such a thing, and whether anything can be done to narrow it. The best advice for neutralizing this so-called gap is for teenagers to confide in their parents and for parents to listen to and advise their teenagers.

Next, discuss the outside influences on teenagers, particularly television and music, and point out the serious responsibility Catholic parents have in guiding their children down the right path, especially when they often have to differ with their friends and neighbors. Teenagers should help parents at these times and not try to go around them or to ridicule them to their friends.

Write the word "authority" on the board and get a correct definition of it. Call attention to the chaos that would exist in society—and that presently exists in some areas—where there is no respect for authority. Parents who couple authority with love and who are firm but fair in enforcing discipline will be respected and loved by their children. The teenage years are difficult and parents and children need each other to get through them unscarred.

Having established the foundation, the catechist may take up the four problem areas of dating, drinking, drugs, and driving. On dating, note that wholesome companionship between boys and girls is normal and good, but there are pitfalls to be avoided. Discuss some ground rules for dating, the dangers of "going steady," and the dead-end street of premarital sex. Emphasize that there are objective standards of morality, such as the Ten Commandments, and that Catholic teenagers must form their consciences accordingly and avoid sinful thoughts, words, and actions, as well as the occasions of sin.

This is an area that is very confused today. Teenagers are being told that anything goes as long as a boy and girl "love" each other. Teachers must present Catholic morality in clear and unmistakable terms. They must also encourage teenagers to strive for purity and to seek divine assistance through prayer, the sacraments, and good works.

Regarding alcohol and narcotic drugs, review the hazards of both, discuss the reasons why teenagers drink or use drugs, and dare them to be different. It would be helpful to have a member of Alcoholics Anonymous or a former drug addict speak to the class about the trouble that can be caused by substance abuse.

The last problem area is driving. Note that a motor vehicle can be a useful tool or a dangerous weapon and an occasion of sin. Have the students visit a rescue squad or the emergency room of a hospital to get some perspective on the carnage that reckless drivers leave behind them. Finally, discuss some ways that a car or truck can help us grow in holiness. Teenagers should be reminded of their responsibility to act as apostles of Christ among their peers.

Topics for Discussion:

1. Is there such a thing as a "generation gap"?
2. What are some outside influences on teenagers?
3. Is "going steady" a good idea?
4. What is the meaning of the statement, "Purity is security"?
5. Why do teenagers drink or experiment with narcotics?
6. What constructive role can teenagers play in modern society?

Some Questions and Answers:

1. How can parental authority be exercised properly?
A. Parental authority must be blended with love if it is to produce a disciplined atmosphere in the family. Teenagers need limits and boundaries, and concerned and loving parents will exercise their authority firmly but fairly, giving their children the flexibility to make some decisions on their own, while at

the same time retaining parental influence and control where necessary.

2. How can parents help teenagers to form a right conscience on sex and dating?
A. As we have mentioned before, parents must first provide their children with positive and prudent sex education. Second, they should discuss moral problems with teenagers, bringing in the moral principles which are found in the Bible and in the teachings of the Church and encouraging chastity and self-control. Third, parents should work out rules for dating with their children, warning them of persons, places, and things which can lead to sin, and discouraging steady dating with one person. Fourth, they should provide an atmosphere where children are concerned with developing their whole personality and not just their sexual powers. Good example by parents can do a lot of good in this area.

3. A friend tells you that he or she is having intercourse, but says that it's all right because they love each other and are practicing "safe sex" with condoms. What should you say?
A. If your friend is not impressed with the fact that premarital sex is contrary to the plan of God and a mortal sin, perhaps he or she will concede that there are a number of practical problems which stem from premarital sex, including the possibility of contracting AIDS or a venereal disease, unwanted pregnancy, and abortion. There is no such thing as "safe sex," except between a husband and wife who are faithful to each other.

Statistics in Linda Thayer's book, *AIDS & Adolescents*, show that condoms have a significant failure rate as a contraceptive and are even less reliable in preventing the spread of the AIDS virus. The statistics also show that providing contraceptive devices and drugs to teenagers has been accompanied by increased rates of adolescent sexual activity, sexually transmitted diseases, and teenage pregnancy. Abstinence from sexual activity—the practice of chastity—is the only effective way to prevent pregnancy and STDs.

If your friend really loves his or her partner, why is he or she willing to expose the loved one to these dangers, not to mention undermining their relationship with God and jeopardizing their eternal salvation? True love means putting the well-being of one's partner first, which your friend does not seem to be doing. Premarital sex is a dead-end street and the signpost reads "Lust" and not "Love."

Projects:

1. Report to the class on the origin of Valentine's Day.
2. Tell your parents that you love and appreciate them.
3. Draw up some ground rules for wholesome dating.
5. Write a paper on the hazards of alcohol and drugs.
6. Volunteer your services at an institution for alcoholics or drug addicts.
7. Visit a hospital emergency room or a fire rescue unit.
8. Pray daily to the Blessed Mother for purity.
9. Set a good example for your peers.

References:

Bonacci, Mary Beth. *Real Love Answers Your Questions on Dating, Marriage, and the Real Meaning of Sex*
Catechism of the Catholic Church
Fox, Fr. Robert J. *The Gift of Sexuality: A Guide for Young People*
John Paul II, Pope. *Familiaris Consortio* ("The Role of the Christian Family in the Modern World")
_____. *Letter to Families*
_____. *Veritatis Splendor* ("The Splendor of Truth")
Kuharski, Mary Ann. *Raising Catholic Children*
Pontifical Council for the Family. *The Truth and Meaning of Human Sexuality*
Pulling, Pat. *The Devil's Web*
Sattler, Vern. *Challenging Children to Chastity*
Thayer, Linda. *AIDS & Adolescents*
U.S. Catholic Conference. *Basic Teachings for Catholic Religious Education*
Vatican II. *Declaration on Christian Education*
_____. *Decree on the Apostolate of the Laity*

Chapter 7

Between Family and Society

Purpose: The purpose of this chapter is to explain the Church's clear and unequivocal opposition to contraception, abortion, and euthanasia.

Tips for Teachers: It would be difficult to find three subjects that are more controversial, more emotional, and less understood than contraception, abortion, and euthanasia. Hence catechists have their work cut out for them in presenting these matters in such a way that the students will see the reasonableness of the Church's rejection of them as means of limiting family size or solving social problems. Take as much time as you need to cover this material fully and to resolve any doubts the students might have.

Begin with a discussion of the anti-life climate that exists in the country today—the manifestations of it, the slogans that are used to disguise the killing ("pro-choice," "death with dignity"), and the threat that this campaign poses to the family and to society. After dealing with in vitro fertilization, the catechist can take up the three major prongs of the anti-life movement.

Define contraception and go over the reasons that are usually offered to justify the practice of artificial birth control, showing how they are not really defensible reasons at all. Point out that the teaching of the Catholic Church against contraception has been constant and unmistakable for nearly two thousand years and has been reaffirmed and restated numerous times in the past seven decades. Have the students read the actual documents in their entirety, particularly *Casti Connubii*, the *Pastoral Constitution on the Church in the Modern World*, *Humanae Vitae*, and *The Role of the Christian Family in the Modern World*, so that they can see the Church's teaching in its full context. Stress the obligation of every Catholic to form his or her conscience according to the teaching of the Church, even when the Pope does not solemnly proclaim that he is making an infallible pronouncement.

Make sure that the students understand that artificial birth control is always immoral and sinful. At the same time, however, draw the distinction between the sin and the sinner, recalling the three conditions for a mortal sin. Point out, too, the evils of contraception for individuals and society. Finally, on a positive note, discuss the Church's teaching on responsible parenthood and the recourse couples may have to natural family planning to space out births for good reasons. Stress the importance of self-control and the divine assistance that is available through prayer and the sacraments. Encourage people to aim for the ideal rather than wallow in mediocrity.

On the question of abortion, the issue is clearer, especially when you can describe what actually happens during pregnancy and illustrate the development of the unborn child with pictures from the books listed under references or with slides and videos that are available from many church and pro-life groups throughout the country. The pictures offer the most convincing argument against abortion, and catechists should make every effort to have their classes see them.

You could also have the students work on a pro-life float for a local parade, make banners with pro-life slogans ("Abortion Stops A Beating Heart," "Give Life A Chance," "Adoption Not Abortion," "It's A Child Not A Choice," "Unborn Babies Are People Too"), join a prayer vigil in front of an abortion facility, or volunteer their time at a place offering alternatives to abortion.

Show how the reasons usually given for abortion are not valid, that no reason can justify killing an innocent unborn baby. Stress that no matter what problem a pregnant girl or woman faces, she should seek help to get rid of the problem and not the baby. Urge the students to get involved in a pro-life group, not only to help fight abortion but also to aid pregnant women in distress. Or suggest that they do volunteer work in institutions for the handicapped or retarded. This is how Christians respond when they are called to holiness.

The last phase of the anti-life movement is the killing of the old and the sick, the retarded and the handicapped, those who are deemed to be of no usefulness to society—whether under the innocent-sounding name of euthanasia or the non-so-innocent term, "assisted suicide." Point out what euthanasia really means and how it is a logical extension of contraception and abortion. Also discuss the true meaning of "death with dignity"; Pope Pius XII's important distinction between ordinary and extraordinary means of prolonging life; the principles contained in the Sacred Congregation for the Doctrine of the Faith's *Declaration on Euthanasia*; our duty to work against laws that would allow the taking of life for social or economic reasons; and our obligation to visit and help care for the sick and the institutionalized.

Topics for Discussion:

1. What are some examples of the anti-life climate or "culture of death" in our country today?
2. Is in vitro fertilization a good idea?
3. Are there any valid reasons for practicing contraception?
4. How many people do you know who would not be alive today if their parents had had only two children? Are you one of those people?
5. Comment on the saying: "Give a man a fish and he will eat for one day; teach him how to fish and he will eat for a lifetime."
6. Do you agree or disagree with Gandhi's statement on contraception?
7. What does the Catholic Church mean by responsible parenthood?
8. Can we say when human life begins?
9. Are there any valid reasons for abortion?
10. Why must life be protected from conception until its natural end?
11. Are there any valid reasons for euthanasia?
12. What is the Christian meaning of "death with dignity"?

Some Questions and Answers:

1. What is wrong with being concerned about the quality of life or whether a person is a useful member of society?

A. For one thing, who decides what the quality of life should be or what it means to be "useful"? If you asked ten people to define "quality of life," you might get ten different answers. One person's idea of a "useful life" might be the complete opposite of another person. Would you want to be placed in one of these categories and marked for extermination on the basis of someone's arbitrary definition of a meaningful life?

Have we already forgotten how the doctors in Nazi Germany tried to raise the quality of life? They started out by killing the severely retarded and handicapped children in institutions and later reduced the price tag on children so low that doctors were killing German children for bed-wetting. They killed people first for medical reasons, then for social reasons, and then for religious reasons.

Once you accept the attitude that there is such a thing as a life not worth living, a life without value, it is but a short step to the "Master Race" (quality race) concept of Hitler. In the eyes of a follower of Christ, all life has quality and meaning because it was created in the image and likeness of God. "Life is a gift from the Creator, to be spent in the service of one's brothers and sisters who, in the plan of salvation, can always draw benefit from it," Pope John Paul said. "It is, therefore, never licit to harm its course, from its beginning to its natural end. Rather, it is to be accepted, respected, and promoted with every means available, and defended from every threat."

2. How do we answer those who say that contraception is necessary to curb a "population explosion" that will use up the world's resources and cause overcrowding and mass starvation?

A. As Jacqueline Kasun has pointed out in her carefully documented book, *The War on Population*, these claims are without foundation. The world has abundant resources and there is no population explosion, particularly not in the United States, where the population has been declining for years. Those countries that are usually cited as critical areas do not have a problem of numbers, but a problem of distribution of the population. They also have failed to develop their resources properly and to pass along to the people the huge quantities of food, aid, and other assistance received from many nations.

Modern technology and agricultural methods could solve the problems of starvation and malnutrition if the governments in underdeveloped lands were less interested in accumulating power and wealth and more interested in the welfare of their citizens. Overcrowding could be relieved by shifting some of the people to less densely populated areas. In other words, there are moral and humane solutions to the problems of poverty and hunger, and Catholics must call attention to them.

3. A priest says that we must always follow our conscience and, if our conscience tells us that artificial birth control is all right, then we are free to practice it. Is this true?

A. No, it is not true, and here are the reasons why. First, every conjugal act must be open to the transmission of life. This teaching has been constantly set forth by the magisterium of the Church and will never change because it is rooted in the nature of man and woman. Second, while the sinfulness of those who practice birth control may be diminished if they are ignorant of or misled about the Church's teaching, or if the full consent of the will is not given, contraception itself is always objectively evil. It is up to the priest in Confession to determine whether the state of mind of the penitent has lessened the sinfulness of the action.

Third, the concept of conscience must be correctly understood. Conscience may be defined as a practical judgment as to whether an action is right or wrong. The key factor, however, is the way in which we arrive at this practical judgment. Do we consider the opinion of friends? Do we consult the advice columns in the newspaper? Do we try to determine what the Church teaches? Do we give equal weight to all of these sources?

The Catholic response to these questions is that our conscience must be formed according to the law of God, as authentically interpreted by the Catholic Church. We are always expected to follow our conscience, but it must be a right conscience, an informed conscience, a conscience that is in tune with the authoritative teaching of the Church, as expressed by the Holy Father. So if one's conscience is contrary to the teaching of the Pope, then one had better reconsider the steps that were taken, and the sources that were consulted, in arriving at an erroneous practical judgment.

4. Since the objective of both artificial contraception and natural family planning is to avoid pregnancy, why does the Church support the natural form when it clearly has the same objective as the artificial means?

A. Both methods do indeed aim to avoid pregnancy, but morally they are not the same. Contraception involves taking direct and deliberate steps before, during, or after the marital act to prevent pregnancy. Natural family planning involves no marital act at all. In other words, contraception means doing something, while NFP means doing nothing.

There's a big difference, morally speaking, between acting against something and not acting at all. In the case of a terminal cancer patient, for example, it would be morally wrong to kill the patient with a drug injection, but it would not be wrong to forego an operation that at best might only keep the patient alive for a short time, that would be very costly financially, and that would cause the patient additional anxiety and suffering.

A couple who for good reasons seeks to practice responsible parenthood by spacing out the births of their children can abstain from marital relations without harboring a hostile and immoral attitude toward human life. They are not attacking life at its very beginning through chemical or mechanical means, but are rather allowing every marital act to remain open to the transmission of life.

Another significant difference between contraception and NFP is that the latter method requires the loving cooperation of both parties instead of placing the burden only on one partner. This mutual involvement of husband and wife, which will demand real communication between them, can enhance the respect, increase the affection, and deepen the love that they feel for each other.

5. Is it true that the Catholic Church once permitted abortion?

A. No, it is not true. The Catholic Church has for two thousand years taught that abortion is always evil. Way back in the first century, in a book of apostolic teachings called the *Didache*, the Church told the faithful: "You shall not procure abortion. You shall not destroy a newborn child."

This condemnation was repeated many times through the centuries by saints and Popes, and was reaffirmed by the Second Vatican Council (1962-1965), which called abortion an "unspeakable crime." The Catholic Bishops of the United States have also denounced the "moral evil of abortion" and have stated that "no Catholic can responsibly take a 'pro-choice' stand when the 'choice' in question involves the taking of innocent human life."

And Pope John Paul II, in *Evangelium Vitae*, used his full authority as the Vicar of Christ on earth to declare that "direct abortion, that is, abortion willed as an end or as a means, always constitutes a grave moral disorder since it is the deliberate killing of an innocent human being" (n. 62).

6. "But if we pass laws forbidding abortion," a friend says, "thousands of women will be forced to put their lives in the hands of back-alley butchers." Please comment.

A. This statement is based on two assumptions: that thousands of women died from illegal abortion prior to its legalization in the United States in 1973, and that illegal abortions are reduced when abortion becomes lawful. Both assumptions are false. In 1973, the year the U.S. Supreme Court struck down all laws against abortion, only 45 women died from illegal abortions, not the "thousands" claimed by the pro-abortionists. But since 1973, scores of women have died from so-called safe, legal abortions, and they will continue to die, and to suffer severe physical and mental complications, because abortion can be a dangerous medical procedure even when performed in an accredited hospital or a licensed clinic.

Second, legalization of abortion does not put an end to illegal procedures. They continue in large numbers because there are several situations where a woman might prefer an illegal abortion. For instance, a married woman who becomes pregnant by another man, or the teenage daughter of a public official, or a woman who does not have the money or the desire to go through the red tape at the local hospital. Thus, even where legal abortions are easily available, some women will still seek illegal ones and suffer the consequences in order to conceal their pregnancy.

And isn't it silly to argue that the best way to prevent the illegal killing of unborn babies is to make it legal to kill them? By the same logic, we can stop such illegal actions as murder, bank robbery, and car theft by making it legal to murder, rob banks, and steal cars.

7. An editorial in a newspaper says that abortion is a Catholic issue and that Catholics have no right to force their moral views on other people. How would you respond?

A. First of all, abortion is not a Catholic issue; it is a human rights and a civil rights issue that is of great concern to people of all religious faiths and of none. As citizens, Catholics have just as much right as anyone else to state their views on public issues, especially on a matter of such grave consequence as the preservation of innocent human life.

But the more important fallacy is the absurd notion that no one should try to impose his moral views on anyone else. Is not this newspaper imposing its moral view on those who are opposed to abortion? Does not virtually every law on our books impose a moral view on someone—on murderers, rapists, thieves, drug pushers?

If this logic were carried to its natural conclusion, you would be expected to watch your next-door neighbor drowning his child in a swimming pool and not do anything about it because you would be accused of forcing your moral views on him. Catholics and others who value human life had better try to persuade a majority of the American people to oppose abortion and euthanasia or no one's life will be safe.

8. What extraordinary means are acceptable to maintain life?

A. This is a difficult question to answer precisely because advances in medicine have changed the definition of what are ordinary and extraordinary means. Furthermore, what the medical profession considers ordinary may be extraordinary to the patient beause of the disproportionate burdens involved. But it is true that surgical procedures once considered extraordinary are now fairly routine. The general principles in these situations were outlined by the Sacred Congregation for the Doctrine of the Faith in its *Declaration on Euthanasia*:

—A patient may choose the latest medical techniques, even if they are risky and still in the experimental stage.

—The patient may halt the use of these advanced techniques if they are not achieving the desired results or if they are imposing on the patient "strain or suffering out of proportion with the benefits which he or she may gain from such techniques."

—One can refuse advanced medical treatment and make do with normal means as an "acceptance of the human condition," to avoid medical procedures disproportionate to the results that can be expected, or to spare the family or the community excessive expenses.

—When death is imminent, the patient can refuse forms of treatment "that would only secure a precarious and burdensome prolongation of life, so long as the normal care due to the sick person in similar cases is not interrupted."

Projects:

1. Report on one of the references listed below.
2. Bring in five clippings from newspapers or magazines showing anti-life bias in the media.
3. Arrange a slide or video presentation on the development of the unborn child or on the methods used by the abortionists to kill a baby.
4. Make pro-life banners or posters or decorate a float.
5. Work with a group that helps women with problem pregnancies.
6. Write to newspapers, radio and TV stations, and sponsors or advertisers, protesting pro-abortion material and requesting equal time for the pro-life side.
7. Write to federal and state lawmakers urging them to pass legislation to protect all life from the womb to the tomb.
8. Volunteer to help in institutions for the handicapped and retarded or visit the old and the sick in hospitals and nursing homes.

References:

Alcorn, Randy. *Pro-Life Answers to Pro-Choice Arguments*
Brennan, William. *The Abortion Holocaust*
Catechism of the Catholic Church
DeMarco, Donald. *Biotechnology and the Assault on Parenthood*
Everett, Carol. *Blood Money: Getting Rich off a Woman's Right to Choose*
John Paul II, Pope. *Evangelium Vitae* ("The Gospel of Life")
_____. *Familiaris Consortio* ("The Role of the Christian Family in the Modern World")
_____. *Letter to Families*
Kasun, Jacqueline. *The War on Population*
Kippley, John F. *Sex and the Marriage Covenant*
_____. and Kippley, Sheila. *The Art of Natural Family Planning*
Lawler, Ronald, Boyle, Joseph, and May, William. *Catholic Sexual Ethics*
Myers, Bishop John J. *The Obligations of Catholics and the Rights of Unborn Children*
Nathanson, Bernard N., M.D. *Aborting America*
_____. *The Hand of God*
O'Connor, John Cardinal. *Abortion: Questions and Answers*
Paul VI, Pope. *Humanae Vitae* ("On Human Life")
Pius XI, Pope. *Casti Connubii* ("On Christian Marriage")
Reardon, David. *Aborted Women: Silent No More*
Rice, Charles E. *50 Questions on Abortion, Euthanasia and Related Issues*
_____. *No Exception: A Pro-Life Imperative*
Rini, Suzanne. *Beyond Abortion: A Chronicle of Fetal Experimentation*
Sacred Congregation for the Doctrine of the Faith. *Declaration on Euthanasia*
_____. *Declaration on Procured Abortion*
_____. *Instruction on Respect for Human Life in Its Origin and on the Dignity of Procreation*
Smith, Herbert F., S.J. *Pro-Choice? Pro-Life?*
Smith, Janet E. *Humanae Vitae: A Generation Later*
Willke, Dr. and Mrs. J. C. *Abortion Questions and Answers*

Chapter 8

Between Family and God

Purpose: The purpose of this chapter is to show the importance to family life of common affection, prayer, work, and recreation.

Tips for Teachers: Start by reminding the students that God's blueprint for the Christian family has been spelled out in various Church documents and that Catholic families ought to do all they can to live according to this blueprint. Discuss the life of Jesus and his family at Nazareth and what it must have been like. Have the students write a short story about an incident that might have happened during the first thirty years of our Lord's life.

Next, talk about the four bonds of family life and how they can unite and strengthen the family. Discuss such things as a proper attitude toward chores, the importance of family prayer and religious articles around the home, and the checklist that indicates a Catholic home. Urge the students to go over this checklist with their families.

Family recreation is also necessary for family togetherness. Have the students discuss the true meaning of recreation and share any ideas from their own family life. Finally, urge them to enjoy their family life while they can.

Topics for Discussion:

1. Why should we look to God for the blueprint of the ideal family?

2. Why do so many people disregard or reject the Church's teaching on marriage and the family?

3. Were the thirty years Jesus spent at Nazareth a waste of time?

4. What can we learn from the life of St. Joseph?

5. What are some ways that your family engages in recreation?

6. How many things on the checklist are a part of your family routine?

Some Questions and Answers:

1. Should children be paid for doing chores?
A. They could be given an allowance so that they will have spending money, but they should not expect to be paid for normal chores at home. The family is a team and every member has to work for the good of the team. This means that each one has certain duties and responsibilities and should carry them out willingly and with a sense of contributing to the well-being of the family. Just as mother does not expect to get paid for cooking the meals or doing the laundry (and others in the family can help with both of these tasks), so children should not expect money for running errands or mowing the lawn.

2. Why is family prayer so important?
A. God must be a part of every Catholic family, and prayer is a way of acknowledging the dependence of the family on God. Furthermore, family prayer cannot help but smooth over any irritations or hard feelings that arise and help draw the family closer together. It is still true that families that pray together generally stay together and are spared many of the problems plaguing so many families today.

3. What are some benefits of family play and recreation?
A. Families who play together learn to understand and enjoy one another. They learn to have fun together, to laugh and romp in a happy atmosphere, to forget the problems and pressures of life. Family recreation can end complaints about boredom, put discipline into perspective, and promote the bond of affection.

Projects:

1. Write a story about an incident that might have occurred during the boyhood of Jesus in Nazareth.
2. Encourage prayer in your family, including grace before and thanks after meals, the Morning Offering, the family rosary, Bible reading, and religious instruction and discussion.

3. Display religious articles and books in your home so that people visiting your house will know that they are in a Catholic home.

4. Set aside one day or night each week for planned family recreation.

5. Invite a lonesome or needy person to your home for dinner or a visit.

6. Introduce the prayers at the end of the chapter to your family.

References:

Catechism of the Catholic Church
John Paul II, Pope. *Christifideles Laici* ("The Lay Members of Christ's Faithful People")
_____. *Familiaris Consortio* ("The Role of the Christian Family in the Modern World")
_____. *Letter to Families*
Kuharski, Mary Ann. *Raising Catholic Children*
Paul VI, Pope. *Humanae Vitae* ("On Human Life")
Pius XI, Pope. *Casti Connubii* ("On Christian Marriage")
Pontifical Council for the Family. *The Truth and Meaning of Human Sexuality*
U.S. Catholic Conference. *Basic Teachings for Catholic Religious Education*
Vatican II. *Decree on the Apostolate of the Laity*
_____. *Dogmatic Constitution on the Church*
_____. *Pastoral Constitution on the Church in the Modern World*
Wilson, Mercedes Arzu. *Love and Family: Raising a Traditional Family in a Secular World*

Chapter 9

The Modern Woman

Purpose: The purpose of this chapter is to show how Christ elevated the status of women and how the women of today ought to pattern themselves after the Blessed Virgin Mary.

Tips for Teachers: Begin the class by discussing the question of equality of women, whether men and women ought to be treated equally, and whether women ought to subscribe to all aspects of the Feminist Movement. This should get a good discussion going and give the catechist an opportunity to point out the degraded status of women before the time of Christ and to show how the Incarnation changed all that. Have the students read the scriptural accounts of the Annunciation and the Visitation and consider their significance for womanhood.

While reading the Bible, do not overlook the wedding feast at Cana as an example of the influence Mary had with Jesus. Even though Jesus was not ready to perform his first miracle, he changed the water into wine because Mary asked him to do so. Other scriptural indications of Jesus' high regard for women include his meeting with the Samaritan woman (John 4:1-26) and his first recorded appearance after the resurrection to a woman, Mary Magadalene (John 20:14-17).

Having demonstrated the way in which Christianity has elevated womanhood, take up the movements in the last century or so that have undermined the true place of women in the family and in society. Particular attention should be paid to Radical Feminism. Note that while women ought to be treated as creatures of God and should never be discriminated against because of their sex, they should be careful not to lose their feminine dignity or to reject their vocation as single women or as mothers devoted to God. Recent papal statements will help women to strike the proper balance between their roles in the family and in society.

Finally, discuss the ideals of womanhood, the profound influence truly Christian women can have on society, and the necessity of imitating Mary, the model for all women. Mary's role as the ideal woman has been spelled out in such Church documents as Pope John Paul's *Mother of the Redeemer* and *On the Dignity and Vocation of Women*. Have the students read both of these important writings of the Holy Father.

Topics for Discussion:

1. What was the status of women before the time of Christ?
2. How did Christ elevate the status of women?
3. Do Mary's words at Cana—"Do whatever he tells you"—have a significance for us today?
4. Are women and men equal in all respects?
5. Has the Radical Feminist Movement benefitted women or not?
6. Should Christian women enter beauty contests?
7. What can be done to make the ideals of womanhood popular today?
8. Should the women of today follow Mary or Eve?
9. Comment on the saying, "The hand that rocks the cradle is the hand that rules the world."

Some Questions and Answers:

1. How do you answer those who say a woman belongs in the home and should not be running around trying to reform society?

A. The primary vocation of a woman is in the home, as a wife and mother. She should perform this vocation to the best of her ability, especially when it comes to the education and training of her children. However, wives and mothers should not be restricted to home-making responsibilities. They can and should make a valuable contribution to society by involving themselves in activities outside the home that affect their family, their parish, and their community.

Of course, neither women nor men should take on so many outside activities that they neglect their first obligation to their family. But the idea that women should hardly ever venture beyond the four walls of their homes is hopelessly out of date today. We all need a change of scenery and varied interests to keep our balance. Women, especially those with large families, should be encouraged to expand their horizons and to spend at least some time outside the home, whether for social, religious, athletic, educational, or cultural reasons.

2. The Blessed Mother seems like such a timid and submissive person. Is she really the best role model for the modern woman?

A. This is a false picture of the Blessed Mother. Consider the full portrait of Mary as painted in the pages of the New Testament:

—She was a woman of intelligence: "How can this be?" she asked the Angel Gabriel (Luke 1:34).

—She was a woman of faith: "Let it be done to me as you say" (Luke 1:38).

—She was a woman of service: Visiting her cousin Elizabeth (Luke 1:39-56).

—She was a woman of courage: Traveling to Bethlehem for the birth of Jesus (Luke 2:4-7) and fleeing into Egypt to escape Herod's wrath (Matthew 2:13-15).

—She was a woman of concern: Searching for Jesus in Jerusalem (Luke 2:41-50).

—She was a woman of contemplation: Pondering things in her memory (Luke 2:19, 51).

—She was a woman of compassion: Helping at the wedding feast in Cana (John 2:1-11).

—She was a woman of influence: "Do whatever he tells you" (John 2:5).

—She was a woman of sorrow: Standing at the cross on Good Friday (John 19:25).

—She was a woman of prayer: Praying with the Apostles (Acts 1:14).

Projects:

1. Read about some of the great woman saints (Catherine of Siena, Joan of Arc, Therese of Lisieux, and Elizabeth Seton) and do a report on the influence they had on society while retaining their feminine qualities.

2. Write a short story about the Blessed Mother based on what Scripture tells us of her life.

3. List five qualities that you think are important in a woman. Which is the most important?

References:

Angelica, Mother. *Mother Angelica's Answers, Not Promises*
Everett, Carol. *Blood Money: Getting Rich off a Woman's Right to Choose*
John Paul II, Pope. *Christifideles Laici* ("The Lay Members of Christ's Faithful People")
_____. *Familiaris Consortio* ("The Role of the Christian Family in the Modern World")
_____. *Letter to Families*
_____. *Mulieris Dignitatem* ("On the Dignity and Vocation of Women")
_____. *Redemptoris Mater* ("Mother of the Redeemer")
Pornography's Victims. Edited by Phyllis Schlafly
Reardon, David C. *Aborted Women: Silent No More*
Steichen, Donna. *Ungodly Rage: The Hidden Face of Catholic Feminism*
Vatican II. *Decree on the Apostolate of the Laity*
_____. *Dogmatic Constitution on the Church*, nos. 52-69
_____. *Pastoral Constitution on the Church in the Modern World*

Chapter 10

The Senior Citizen

Purpose: The purpose of this chapter is to gain a clearer understanding of the senior citizens among us and what can be done to help them get the most out of their twilight years.

Tips for Teachers: There are two major aspects of this chapter to be covered—what the younger generation can do to help the elderly and what the elderly can do to help themselves. First, remind the students of their obligation to care for old and sick parents. Point out, too, that the young can learn a great deal from the elderly and should take advantage of the opportunity to work with them and care for them.

Discuss next how the elderly can carry on an active apostolate in their community, and a deeply spiritual one, too. There are unlimited ways in which senior citizens can provide service to others, and they should be encouraged to get involved, both for their own good and the well-being of those with whom they come into contact. Age need not be a barrier to this service, as history has shown.

We all need to be needed, especially as we grow older, and the students must be made aware of the loneliness experienced by the elderly. Companionship and conversation are important to senior citizens, and the younger generation can perform real works of Christian charity by providing both.

Take up the observations and suggestions of the Little Sisters of the Poor. Their insights are extremely important if we are to understand the situation of the elderly, either as lay persons or, for women, as Little Sisters of the Poor. Catechists should encourage young women to consider a vocation with the Little Sisters.

Topics for Discussion:

1. Do children have an obligation to care for their parents?
2. What can the younger generation learn from senior citizens?

3. What is the greatest problem facing the elderly?
4. What can you do to help senior citizens cope with their problems?
5. Who are some people of advanced age that are still making important contributions to society?
6. What are some of the reasons for institutionalizing the elderly?
7. Why do so many senior citizens die in their first year in an institution?

Some Questions and Answers:

1. A friend says that his father is in a nice nursing home, with all the conveniences and comforts one could want, but he is always complaining. What can you say?

A. Tell your friend that all the material comforts in the world cannot make up for his father's sense of loneliness and his feeling that no one really cares about him. What the father needs is love and affection, companionship and concern, and the realization that his life still has some meaning. In addition to giving money to the nursing home for his father's expenses, your friend should also give some of himself to his father.

2. Wasn't there a humorous poem that the late Richard Cardinal Cushing used to recite to give senior citizens some enjoyment and consolation?

A. The late Archbishop of Boston, who suffered from a variety of ailments, once composed a cheerful and inspirational poem about his physical problems. The B.C. referred to in the poem is Boston College, the Cardinal's *alma mater*.

I'M FINE!

I live out in Brighton, close to B.C.
And I'm just as healthy as I can be.
I have arthritis in both knees,
And when I must speak, I talk with a wheeze.
My pulse is weak and my blood is quite thin
But I'm awfully well for the shape that I'm in.

I need arch supporters to strengthen my feet,
My ankles are swollen, I'm white as a sheet.
I toss in my bed without sleep every night;
No wonder each morning I look like a sight.
My memory is failing, my head's in a spin,
But I'm awfully well for the shape that I'm in.

Diverticulitis is a word hard to spell,
But it's a disease from which I'll never get well.
Ulcers that keep me on a diet of Maalox
Prevent me from resting in a funeral box.
The length of my sermons brings yawns or a grin,
But I'm awfully well for the shape that I'm in.

The moral is, friends, as this tale I unfold,
That for you and me who are fast growing old
It's better to say, "I'm fine," with a grin,
Than to let people know of the shape that we're in.

Projects:

1. Invite an active senior citizen to speak to the class.
2. Visit a senior citizen on a regular basis, either in your neighborhood or at a nursing home.
3. Ask a senior citizen for advice or help with a problem.
4. Encourage them to become active letter writers.
5. Arrange a dinner or an outing for a group of senior citizens in your parish or community.

References:

John Paul II, Pope. *Christifideles Laici* ("The Lay Members of Christ's Faithful People")

_____. *Familiaris Consortio* ("The Role of the Christian Family in the Modern World")

_____. *Letter to Families*

_____. *Salvifici Doloris* ("On the Christian Meaning of Human Suffering")

Chapter 11

The Eighth Person

Purpose: The purpose of this chapter is to encourage students to reject all discrimination based on sex, race, color, religion, language, or social conditions as contrary to the teachings of Christ and his Church, and to remind them of their Christian obligation to apply the principles of social justice in their lives.

Tips for Teachers: The catechist could begin by asking for examples of racial, religious, or sex discrimination in the United States, particularly in the community where the students live. The most common examples involve blacks, Jews, and women, but there are also increasing acts of discrimination against Catholics and other Christians who take a strong stand against abortion and homosexual behavior.

After reviewing the Church's teaching against this kind of prejudice, beginning with St. Paul and continuing up through recent Popes, recall the conversion of Paul and Christ's statement that persecution of his followers was the same as persecution of him. Read and discuss Christ's account of the Last Judgment and his warning that we will be judged on how we treated the least of our brothers and sisters.

Another important area to cover is the tendency people have to blame a whole race or religious group for the faults of a few of its members. Stress that no one race or religion has a monopoly on good or evil, that there are saints and sinners in all groups. Draw a distinction, too, between the sin and sinner; we must love the sinner while hating the sin. We are also expected to love our neighbor, that is, to treat him or her as a brother or sister in Christ, even though we may not particularly like our neighbor. Having the same Father in heaven makes all of us brothers and sisters.

In working for social justice, the students should be cautioned to avoid the extremes of doing nothing or becoming a wild-eyed militant who is willing to trample on the rights of some people to secure the rights of others. Knowledge of the issues and prudence in pursuing a solution to them are necessary qualities for Christian apostles. We can "make the time ripe" by not trying to change the world in a week, but rather by working for these goals patiently and persistently among our families and friends, in our community and country.

The "Serenity Prayer" contains some good advice:

> God grant me the serenity to accept the things that I cannot change, courage to change the things that I can, and wisdom to know the difference.

The other point to be reiterated is that we leave a lot of good things undone. It is important for us to avoid doing evil, but it is also important for us to act in a positive and constructive way to alleviate injustice and combat hatred. We must live like faithful Catholics all during the week, not just at Mass on Saturday evening or Sunday morning. How can one receive the Holy Eucharist at Mass and then go out and treat people unjustly?

The catechist should explain the doctrine of the Mystical Body and show how the Mass unites us with our fellow Catholics all over the world. If we believe in this unity, if we really love God, then we will also love our neighbor and do all we can to help him or her, especially when they are in need.

Throughout the Mass there are reminders of our unity with one another. At the Offertory, for instance, we offer up our gifts and petitions to God as a community; at the Consecration, we are reminded that Christ died for all people, and not just for one race or religion. The Holy Eucharist is the sacrament of unity, and students should be encouraged to receive it with this in mind. Take the time to go through the Mass with the class, using the missalettes that many parishes have, and have the boys and girls pick out the prayers and actions that relate to our unity.

Finally, talk about the absurdity of prejudice and how we must use our time, talent, and influence to fight discrimination and to aid our brothers and sisters in Christ to achieve their dignity as human beings. Review the principles regarding the dignity of the individual—our natural and supernatural unity, our basic equality, our right to life. All of these must be respected and protected.

THE EIGHTH PERSON 67

A poem by an unknown author summarizes the chapter well:

A man's no bigger than the way he treats his fellow man.
This standard has been his measure since time itself began.
He's measured not by tithes or creed, high-sounding though they be;
Nor by the gold he's put aside, not by his capacity.
He's measured not by social rank, when character's the test,
Nor by his earthly pomp or show, displaying wealth possessed.
He's measured by his justice, right, his fairness at his play,
His squareness in all dealings made, his honest, upright way.
These are his measures ever near to serve him when they can
For no man's bigger than the way he treats his fellow man.

Topics for Discussion:

1. Is there a discrimination problem in America?
2. If we say "Our Father," are we not all brothers and sisters?
3. When was the last time you gave food to the hungry or drink to the thirsty or clothes to the naked or welcome to a stranger?
4. How can you "make the time ripe" for social justice?
5. Comment on the saying, "One does evil by not doing any good."
6. Discuss the following verse: "Mr. Jones went to church; he never missed a Sunday. But Mr. Jones went to hell for what he did on Monday."
7. Can a person be a good Catholic and practice racial or religious prejudice?

Some Questions and Answers:

1. A friend says that when she heard a black family was moving into the neighborhood, "I almost died. I won't be able to sleep at night knowing how many blacks are involved in violent crimes." What would you say to her?
A. Tell her that she is wrong in prejudging all blacks on the basis of the actions of some blacks. Every race and reli-

gion has its share of good and bad people, and it is unfair and un-Christian to blame a whole group for the sins of a few members.

2. Another friend knows that he is supposed to love his neighbor, but he says, "You don't know my neighbor. He's a drunken bum who has parties all night and we often have to call the police. How can I love someone like that?" What should your response be?

A. Love of neighbor does not mean that you have to like your neighbor or put up with riotous and immoral conduct from him. Christ loved the Pharisees, but this did not prevent him from denouncing their hypocrisy. He loved the money-changers, but this did not stop him from angrily chasing them out of the temple. We have to distinguish, as Christ did, between the sin and sinner. We can detest what our neighbor is doing while at the same time praying for him and, if the opportunity arises, trying to persuade him to change his life. It will not be easy, but a good Christian will make a valiant effort anyway. That's what it means to love your neighbor.

3. What is the Mystical Body of Christ?

A. The Mystical Body of Christ refers to the Church of which Christ is the head, and the faithful, living and dead, are the members. The doctrine, which stems from Christ's statement, "I am the vine, you are the branches" (John 15:5), describes the real and spiritual union which the faithful have with Christ and with their brothers and sisters. "By communicating his Spirit to his brothers, called together from all peoples, Christ made them mystically into his own body," said the Second Vatican Council. "In that body, the life of Christ is poured into the believers who, through the sacraments, are united in a hidden and real way to Christ who suffered and was glorified" (*Dogmatic Constitution on the Church*, n. 7).

In the same paragraph, the Council also said that this unity, sustained by the Holy Eucharist, is such that "if one member suffers anything, all the members suffer it too, and if one member is honored, all the members rejoice together (cf. 1 Corinthians 12:26)." See also the *Catechism of the Catholic Church*, nn. 787-795.

4. What are the specific duties of a Christian towards his neighbor?

A. In their document entitled *Basic Teachings for Catholic Religious Education*, the Bishops of the United States gave this answer:

Towards his fellow man the Christian has specific obligations in love. Like Christ, he will show that love by concern for the rights of his fellow man—his freedom, his housing, his food, his health, his right to work, etc. The Christian is to show all others the justice and charity of Christ—to reach out in a spirit of the Beatitudes to help all others, to build up a better society in the local community and justice and peace throughout the world. His judgment and speech concerning others are to be ruled by the charity due all sons of God. He will respect and obey all lawful authority in the home, in civil society, and in the Church.

Projects:

1. Make posters stressing the theme of love of neighbor.

2. Write an essay on brotherhood' or sisterhood.

3. Arrange a panel discussion with different races and religions represented.

4. Sponsor an interracial or interreligious prayer meeting in your church or school.

5. Sponsor a "Brotherhood Week" in your community.

6. Pray often and especially at Mass for an end to discrimination and prejudice.

7. Perform a corporal or spiritual work of mercy at least once a week.

References:

Catechism of the Catholic Church

Catholic League for Religious and Civil Rights. *Pius XII and the Holocaust*

John Paul II, Pope. *Christifideles Laici* ("The Lay Members of Christ's Faithful People")

_____. *Mulieris Dignitatem* ("On the Dignity and Vocation of Women")

_____. *Sollicitudo Rei Socialis* ("On Social Concern")

John XXIII, Pope. *Pacem in Terris* ("Peace on Earth")
Paul VI, Pope. *Populorum Progressio* ("On the Development of Peoples")
Pius XII, Pope. *Mystici Corporis* ("The Mystical Body")
Rader, Fr. John S., and Fedoryka, Kateryna. *The Pope and the Holocaust*
U.S. Catholic Conference. *Basic Teachings for Catholic Religious Education*
_____. *Brothers and Sisters to Us: U.S. Bishops' Pastoral Letter on Racism in Our Day*
_____. *Sharing the Light of Faith: National Catechetical Directory for Catholics of the United States*
Vatican II. *Declaration on the Relationship of the Church to Non-Christian Religions*
_____. *Dogmatic Constitution on the Church*
_____. *Pastoral Constitution on the Church in the Modern World*

Chapter 12

Christian Stewardship

Purpose: The purpose of this chapter is to instill in the students a proper understanding of and correct attitude towards Christian stewardship.

Tips for Teachers: You can start this class with the following story. A few years ago, a tornado roared through the Midwest and left substantial damage in its wake. A Catholic church in one town had its roof torn off and the walls were in bad shape. As a group of parishioners picked their way through the rubble inside the church, they noticed that a statue of the Sacred Heart, with arms extended, was still standing. The only apparent damage was that both of our Lord's hands were missing.

As the people came closer to the statue, they saw that someone had left a hand-lettered sign leaning against it. The sign read: "I have no hands but yours."

This is what Christian stewardship is all about. There are many people—in our communities, in our country, in our world—who are lacking the necessities of life. They have no hands but ours. The teacher must define and explain what stewardship means, how vital it is for a Christian and for the Church, and how misunderstood and ignored this concept is today. We have an obligation to share with others the material blessings that God has given to us. Read and discuss the parables mentioned in the chapter, particularly the one about the silver pieces, to see just how clear this teaching of Jesus is.

There are countless ways that we can share with other people. Ask the students for some concrete examples and urge them to carry out their suggestions. Emphasize, too, that sometimes the giving of yourself is more important than just giving material things. Visiting with a poor person can sometimes do more good for their morale than gifts of money.

You can illustrate the value of giving of yourself with "The Legend of the 19 Camels." It goes like this. There was an Arab man who died and left an estate of nineteen camels. His will specified that the estate should be divided, with one-half going to his wife, one-quarter to his older son, and one-fifth to his younger son. Nineteen is not divisible by one-half, one-fourth, or one-fifth, and so the family was soon involved in a bitter argument over each one's share of the estate.

While the argument was raging, a friend arrived to pay his respects to the family. He listened to the squabbling for a few minutes and then went outside, where he untied his own camel, took it around back, and put it with the nineteen camels. He called the family outside and told each one to take his share. The widow took half, ten camels; the older son took one-fourth, five camels; and the younger son took one-fifth, four camels. The visitor then mounted his own camel and rode away.

By adding his own camel to make twenty, the friend had solved the problem. He did not have to give up his own camel, or to give away anything of a material nature. He simply gave of himself and, by putting himself in the middle of a difficult situation, he was able to do a great service for the family. Remind the students that there will be times in their lives when they will be able to assist and serve others just by giving of themselves.

One essential aspect of stewardship is support for one's parish and for the Church near and far. This support should include financial contributions as well as volunteering of time and talent. Our parishes provide a lot of support for us, primarily spiritual, and we have an obligation in justice to help the parish. We should be as generous as we can, even sacrificing to help others in desperate circumstances.

Our weekly offering can not only aid the parish in meeting its expenses, but it can be a significant gesture of thanks to God for all he has done for us. Giving students a proper perspective on parish giving will aid the Church in the future.

Make sure that the students understand that we will be judged by God on our stewardship, on our use of the time, talent, and earthly goods he has given to us. God will want to know how well we acted as our brother's and sister's keeper. Have the students give an account of their own personal stewardship, using the standards suggested at the end of the chapter in the text.

Topics for Discussion:

1. What do we mean by Christian stewardship?
2. Are you using to the fullest the talents God gave you?
3. Must we share with others only on the basis of our surplus, or should we give from our necessary income when we discover others in more need than us?
4. Can we be stingy with the God who has been so generous to us?
5. Do you profess your faith without practicing it?
6. Is it right to claim an income tax deduction that is larger than what you actually gave to the Church?
7. Should you tithe, that is, give ten percent or some other fixed percentage of your income to the parish every week?

Some Questions and Answers:

1. What does it mean to be in the world but not of the world?
A. It means that we must not become too attached to the things of this world; that we are pilgrims on a journey through this life and that our ultimate goal will only be achieved in the next life; that while we have an obligation to assist our fellow pilgrims on the road to heaven, we must not get too caught up in the temporal pleasures of this world lest we forget that they are as nothing compared to the eternal joys of heaven. "What profit would a man show," Jesus asked, "if he were to gain the whole world and destroy himself in the process?" (Matthew 16:26).

2. A friend says that he puts money in the Offertory collection every week at Mass and that is all he has to do to support his parish. Is he right?
A. No, he is not right. He is to be commended for his financial contributions—many Catholics don't even do that—but there is much more that he can do. For instance, he could be an usher, lector, or extraordinary minister. He could teach CCD or help the religious education program in some other capacity. He could coach school or parish sports teams, become active in parish organizations, ring a few doorbells for

the parish census or a fundraising appeal, do odd jobs around the parish property, or perhaps advise the pastor on major repairs or renovations that might be necessary. Lay people have a certain expertise that parish priests do not have, and they can offer valuable service to their parish by coming forward with their ideas and their willingness to work.

3. A friend complains that the priests are always asking for money and says that such appeals do not belong in church. What would you say?
A. Your friend should sit down with the pastor some day and see what it costs to run a parish. Do the church and rectory, school and hall maintain themselves? Is the gas or oil or electricity free? Home expenses have increased substantially in recent years. Does your friend think that the parish has been spared these increased expenses?

Perhaps some priests do talk too much about money. If your friend feels this way, why doesn't she approach the pastor with some ideas on how to raise money so that the appeals from the pulpit could be limited to one or two a year.

In any case, giving money to one's parish is part of being a faithful steward. It is a sharing of our gifts with others. In the early Church, people brought up food at the Offertory; now we contribute money, but the principle is the same. Speaking of food, perhaps your parish could start a "food pantry" or clothing collection to gather items for poor families. This would be a wonderful example of stewardship.

Projects:

1. Write an essay on what your parish could do to reach out to those in need.
2. Take one of the parables mentioned in the chapter and write a modern-day story emphasizing the same theme.
3. Thank God every day for all he has given to you and ask him for guidance in using your talents and possessions in his service and that of your brothers and sisters in Christ.
4. Take some of the suggestions under "What Can We Share" and put them into practice immediately.
5. Volunteer your services to the Church.

References:

Catechism of the Catholic Church
John Paul II, Pope. *Christifideles Laici* ("The Lay Members of Christ's Faithful People")
_____. *Sollicitudo Rei Socialis* ("On Social Concern")
John XXIII, Pope. *Mater et Magistra* ("Christianity and Social Progress")
Paul VI, Pope. *Populorum Progressio* ("On the Development of Peoples")
Vatican II. *Decree on the Apostolate of the Laity*
_____. *Pastoral Constitution on the Church in the Modern World*

Chapter 13

Morality in Public Life

Purpose: The purpose of this chapter is to review the moral principles which ought to be paramount in public and political life.

Tips for Teachers: Morality in politics is very much in the news these days so here is a chance to get the students thinking about the need for people with moral integrity in public life. Polls taken from time to time show that people have less and less confidence in their political and governmental leaders. Ask the students for their opinion on whether politicians can be believed and trusted and use the results for a discussion of the three basic principles or qualities that ought to be found in any suitable candidate for public office: required knowledge, moral integrity, and willingness to accept the office.

Once such a candidate has been located, he or she ought to be supported and, if elected, given plenty of encouragement and praise for trying to do a difficult job well. We often write to public officials to criticize something they have done, but we seldom give them a pat on the back for doing something that we think is right.

Going from the positive to the negative, the catechist must bring up the huge problem of graft and bribery in political life—from the national level down to the local and precinct level. Stress that public office is a public trust and that graft and bribery are immoral and sinful no matter how many people are doing it or how acceptable it has become (cf. *Catechism of the Catholic Church*, n. 2409).

Catholic officeholders must shoot for the ideal and set a good example. They should try to raise the level of morality instead of helping to lower it. They should travel the road of integrity, not the road of dishonesty and mediocrity. The art of being honest is becoming a lost art today, and the students must be made to realize that they have a Christian obligation to restore this art to public life. They must realize, too, that this will not be accomplished overnight, that it will take a lot of hard work and will involve abuse from those who have a vested interest in dishonesty. If they do not think they will be able to stand the heat, they should stay out of the kitchen.

Also to be discussed in this class is the avoidance of slander or detraction during or between political campaigns. When a candidate is smeared by an opponent, the natural reaction is to respond in kind, but Catholic candidates must resist this temptation to get down in the gutter with their opponents. There should be no violation of secrecy or the confidences of another person either.

The final point to be stressed is that morality in public life involves not only seeking and holding public office but, for the majority of citizens, taking an active interest in the issues and the people running and then getting out to vote on election day. It has been said that people get the kind of government and public officials they deserve, meaning that if you do not study the candidates and if you stay home on election day, you really cannot complain when things are not done the way you think they should be done.

The decisions made by public officials affect every facet of our lives, so it is rather important that we elect people who will reflect Catholic values and principles. Only an informed, conscientious, and God-fearing electorate can make this truly one nation under God.

Topics for Discussion:

1. Can politicians be believed and trusted?

2. Does separation of church and state mean that religious and moral principles have no place in political life?

3. What are the most important qualities to look for in a candidate for public office?

4. Are you a "practical" Catholic or a "practicing" Catholic?

5. Do those who have no interest in politics and government have a right to criticize and berate those who are willing to stand on the firing line?

6. Should Catholics support candidates whose views on some issues—abortion, divorce, homosexuality—are contrary to the teaching of Jesus and his Church?

7. Is there anything wrong with taking a useless or easy government job as a reward for party loyalty?

Some Questions and Answers:

1. Where can Catholic office seekers find the moral principles that they need to know to serve their constituents well?
A. Primarily from the *Catechism of the Catholic Church* (nn. 1886-1927), the social encyclicals of the Popes, some of which are listed under references, and from Vatican II's *Pastoral Constitution on the Church in the Modern World*. Catholic government officials might also read about St. Thomas More (cf. the movie *A Man for All Seasons*), who gave up his life rather than endorse the immoral actions of his King. Just before he was beheaded, Thomas said, "I die the King's good servant, but God's first." Another source of inspiring examples of moral and political courage for those in public office is John F. Kennedy's book, *Profiles in Courage*, which tells the stories of some Americans who put principle above political party.

2. A politician tells you that "we have to cut corners here and there and compromise on some of our principles if we expect to accomplish anything in office." How would you respond?
A. What the politician is really saying is that the end justifies the means—a theory that is unacceptable to any morally sound person. Once you give in on one principle, and then on another, you begin to lose your moral bearings. The principles that are discarded become more and more significant, the compromises become greater and greater, and soon a person becomes interested only in preserving his political position and perquisites. He or she has become so intent on doing the expedient thing, rather than the right thing, and has incurred so many political debts to so many people, that they are no longer able to do much good in public office.

Projects:

1. Read about St. Thomas More and report to the class.

2. Read one of the stories in *Profiles in Courage* and report to the class.

3. Read one of the papal encyclicals or Church documents mentioned below and list five moral principles that Catholic public officials should follow.

4. Invite a Catholic politician of known integrity to speak to the class.

5. Write a letter to or visit one of your state or federal representatives and let them know how you feel about some important issue.

6. Work and vote for good political candidates.

7. Enter politics yourself and try to raise the moral tone.

8. Pray every day for those in public life.

9. Be honest and truthful in all you do.

References:

Catechism of the Catholic Church
Connell, Francis J. *Morals in Politics and Professions*
Kennedy, John F. *Profiles in Courage*
John Paul II, Pope. *Christifideles Laici* ("The Lay Members of Christ's Faithful People")
_____. *Sollicitudo Rei Socialis* ("On Social Concern")
Pope John XXIII, Pope. *Mater et Magistra* ("Christianity and Social Progress")
_____. *Pacem in Terris* ("Peace on Earth")
Vatican II. *Decree on the Apostolate of the Laity*
_____. *Pastoral Constitution on the Church in the Modern World*

Chapter 14

Cults and the New Age Movement

Purpose: The purpose of this chapter is to demonstrate the nature of destructive religious movements and the danger of getting involved in them.

Tips for Teachers: Start by asking the class what the word "cult" means to them, and then go over the definition of a destructive cult that appears on page 184 of the text, explaining each of the five parts of the definition. You can also suggest using Fr. Gesy's yardstick to determine whether a new religious movement is destructive.

Next ask the students why they think a person would join a cult. Perhaps one or more members of the class might even have some personal experience in this matter. In any case, talk about the most common reasons and have the students suggest ways of dealing with the problems and difficulties that could make a person vulnerable to cult recruiters.

There are four types of religious movements, according to Cardinal Arinze, and they can be distinguished by certain characteristics. List the movements, and their characteristics, on the board or on flash cards and mention some of the specific groups that might be included in each category. Refer to the Gesy, LeBar, Steffon, and Pacwa books for further information.

The remainder of the class should focus on the three general categories of cults: witchcraft, satanism, and the New Age Movement. The principal beliefs of each are summarized in the text, but familiarity with the authors mentioned above, as well as with Donna Steichen's book *Ungodly Rage*, will be helpful to the catechist.

Wicca or witchcraft is thought by many to be a benign or harmless activity, as indicated by the belief system agreed upon by the Council of American Witches in 1974 (cf. page 187). But point out that, at best, their practices leave them open to evil influences, as made clear by the letter from a former witch that appears on pages 188-189.

Satanism is the most destructive of the destructive religious movements because it is in close contact with the father of evil himself. Watch for news reports of satanic rituals, and point out the dangers of fooling with seances, ouija boards, and such fantasy role-playing games as "Dungeons & Dragons." See Pat Pulling's book *The Devil's Web* for further details. If the class is mature enough, the catechist could bring in *The Satanic Bible* and *The Satanic Rituals*, but they must be used with caution and prudence.

List the five levels of satanism described by Fr. Steffon, discuss some of the things that attract people to satanic cults, and review some of the signs of satanic involvement. Finally, have the students memorize the prayer to St. Michael and urge them to say it every day.

The last major category involves the many-faceted New Age Movement, which is a blend of some Eastern religions, ancient heresies, and modern Western occultism and mind-control techniques. Try to define as many of the terms as you can (there are excellent glossaries at the back of Fr. Steffon's and Fr. Pacwa's books) so the students will have some idea of the actual meaning of such things as astral projection, pantheism, channeling, crystals, and nirvana.

Make clear that the beliefs of the New Age Movement are in no way compatible with Christianity, that theories such as reincarnation have been condemned by St. Paul, and that its various practices of divination, its reliance on mediums to the spirit world, and its fascination with astrology, horoscopes, and palm reading are contrary to the First Commandment, which says that we must always put God first by paying him the adoration and respect due to the Creator of the universe.

Touch on Enneagrams as another New Age fad and note their occult origins as spelled out in the Pacwa book. Finally, take up the suggestions for combatting the New Age Movement that are offered by Fr. Pacwa, and call attention to the many individuals and organizations listed at the back of the Pacwa, LeBar, and Gesy books that can help those who are caught up in destructive religious movements.

Topics for Discussion:

1. What is a cult?
2. What makes a cult destructive?
3. Why do people join cults?
4. Is witchcraft a harmless activity?
5. What are some signs of satanic influence?
6. Is reincarnation a possibility?
7. Why is it wrong to take part in seances or to consult astrologers, horoscopes, or palm readers?

Some Questions and Answers:

1. What are the dangers of playing "Dungeons & Dragons"?

A. In chapter 5 of his book *Satanism: Is It Real?*, Fr. Jeffrey Steffon summarizes the dangers of the fantasy role-playing employed in D&D:

> From a Christian perspective, D&D can be a dangerous game. Its philosophical basis is contrary to the Christian worldview. D&D tends to be graphically violent in its fantasy play. It can also be dangerous because it may intensify psychological problems in some players, or may even be linked to an act of violence by some troubled teenagers ....
>
> D&D can be dangerous because it may become an entrance into the occult through its teachings and practice of magic and witchcraft. Inasmuch as it treats Christ as a fantasy character and as one among many gods, D&D may undermine the faith of Christians who play it. For a follower of Jesus Christ, there is no good reason to role-play fantasy characters who regularly practice magic and witchcraft which God condemns (pp. 71-72).

2. How reliable are Enneagrams?

A. They are not reliable because there may be more than the nine personality types shown on the circular diagram used with Enneagrams, and because they lead those involved to make subjective judgments about the personalities of other people. There is nothing scientific about them and they are certainly not useful as tools for spiritual direction since there are so many non-Christian elements mixed in. Methods of prayer or spiritual exercises that are not inspired by Christ and that do not lead back to him are not valid for the Christian man or woman. That is why followers of Christ should stay away from Enneagrams.

3. How can young people be protected from cults?

A. Cults usually fill a void in a person's life — a lack of love or friends or a strong spiritual faith. So the obvious way to deflect cultic influences is, first, to build up the religious faith of young people through solid instruction and explanations of what Catholics believe and why they believe those things. An active prayer life, frequent recourse to the sacraments, Bible reading, and devotion to the Blessed Mother will strengthen anyone against evil influences.

Parents, relatives, friends, and other young people who already possess a firm faith should reach out to those who are floundering or who are looking for some meaning to life and for someone who cares about them. The vulnerable jump into cults because they think they will find there what is missing in their lives. If their families or friends were already making efforts to help them and to show love and concern for them, many young people would not be ripe for plucking by cultists seeking power over them.

Projects:

1. Prepare a poster on the dangers of cults.
2. Assign students to do a report on one destructive religious movement discussed in the reference books listed below.
3. Plan a prayer service built around the prayer to St. Michael the Archangel.
4. Demonstrate that Jesus is God, not just another spiritual guide (see chapter 6 of *Catholicism and Reason*, a companion volume in this series, for some good evidence).
5. Arrange a speaking program about cults.

References:

Catechism of the Catholic Church
Gesy, Fr. Lawrence J. *Today's Destructive Cults and Movements*
LeBar, Fr. James J. *Cults, Sects and the New Age*
Pacwa, Mitch, S.J. *Catholics and the New Age*
Pulling, Pat. *The Devil's Web*
Steffon, Fr. Jeffrey J. *Satanism: Is It Real?*
Steichen, Donna. *Ungodly Rage: The Hidden Face of Catholic Feminism*

Chapter 15

Advocates of Atheism

Purpose: The purpose of this chapter is to acquaint the students with the origins and spread of organized atheism.

Tips for Teachers: The subject of atheism or Marxism-Leninism is an extensive one, involving ideology, history, strategy and tactics, and the often-inadequate response to this movement that changed the history of the twentieth century. In the pages of the text, we could do little more than scratch the surface of what Catholics ought to know about this evil force. The many references listed in this manual will be helpful in gaining a greater understanding of how it took the lives of more than one hundred million men, women, and children in less than a century.

Some changes have taken place in recent years in what was once the Soviet empire but, as these words are written, it is still too soon to tell how far-reaching and authentic the changes are and whether they will lead to real freedom and justice for our brothers and sisters in those lands. Whatever the future brings, however, it is worth reviewing the basic principles of Marxism-Leninism and studying some of the key personalities responsible for its spread around the globe.

Assign the students outside research on Marx, Engels, Lenin, and Gorbachev and have them report to the class. Once these men are better known, it will be easier to understand the way of life they devised and/or put into operation. Information could also be gathered on other key figures in the rise of communism, including Joseph Stalin, Nikita Khrushchev, and Leonid Brezhnev in the former Soviet Union, Mao Tse-tung and Chou En-lai in Communist China, Ho Chi Minh in North Vietnam, and Fidel Castro in Cuba.

Topics for Discussion:

1. What is atheism and what is wrong with it?
2. What do you think prompted people to become communists or Marxist-Leninists?

3. Who were some of the leaders of this movement during the past century?

Some Questions and Answers:

1. I can remember communist rulers coming to the United States and talking about world peace and getting along together. Why didn't more people try to meet them halfway and end the Cold War sooner?

A. Some people accepted the communists at their word and tried to reach fair agreements with them, but they soon found out that words like "peace" and "liberation" and "detente" had quite different meanings to the communists than to most people. To the communists "peace" meant not the absence of fighting but rather that state of affairs when there was no longer any opposition to communism; "liberation" meant not restoring freedom to a country but rather imposing Marxism-Leninism on the country; and "detente" meant not working toward peace and harmony between nations but rather gaining one-sided concessions that would put the United States at a disadvantage in such areas as arms control and disarmament.

Father Stephen Dunker, the Vincentian missionary who spent many years in Communist Chinese prisons, put it this way:

> Communists are criminal conspirators who use words and slogans as weapons in their total war against us. When the communists cry "peace," they really mean they want to conquer the world one piece at a time. When the communists invite us to "peaceful coexistence," they mean they want us to coexist as the man on the gallows coexists with the rope around his neck.

Another reason why many people were skeptical about communist words was that their actions contradicted what they were saying. While they talked about peace, their armies and secret police were killing and jailing people not only in the Soviet Union, but also in many other nations. That figure of more than one hundred million murdered is no exaggeration, and the killing took place while communist rulers were smiling and talking about peaceful coexistence.

2. But wasn't most of that killing done by Lenin and Stalin in the 1920s, 1930s, and 1940s? Didn't those kinds of actions pretty much stop in recent decades?
A. The bulk of the one hundred million deaths did occur under Lenin and Stalin, and under Mao Tse-tung and Chou En-Lai in China, but millions also perished under Khrushchev, Brezhnev, Andropov, and Gorbachev in the 1950s, 1960s, 1970s, and 1980s. Soviet troops slaughtered three million people in Afghanistan during the 1980s, not the 1930s. And the Chinese communist rulers massacred thousands of peaceful student protesters in Beijing as recently as the summer of 1989.

3. Didn't a lot of countries fall to communism because they were poor? Would the situation have been different if we could have helped those people overcome hunger and poverty?
A. This so-called stomach theory of communism is false. Of course, we should do all we can to help alleviate hunger and poverty, but communism was forced on those countries from the top down. It was never imposed by those in poverty but rather by those who were well-off and more interested in power than in helping the poor. The most successful Marxist-Leninists in this century were Lenin, Stalin, Gorbachev, Mao, Chou, Ho Chi Minh, and Castro—none of whom was poor or downtrodden.

Projects:

1. Read a basic study of communism and report to the class.
2. Read Pope Pius XI's encyclical on Atheistic Communism and report to the class.
3. Prepare biographical sketches of some of the key Marxist-Leninists since 1917.
4. Pay attention to what is going on in Russia, China, Cuba, and other countries and see what progress is being made toward freedom and justice for the people.

References:

Barron, John, and Paul, Anthony. *Murder of a Gentle Land*
Carroll, Warren. *70 Years of the Communist Revolution*

Carson, Clarence. *Basic Communism: Its Rise, Spread and Debacle in the 20th Century*
Chamberlin, William H.. *The Russian Revolution* (2 vols.)
Chambers, Whittaker. *Witness*
Conquest, Robert. *The Great Terror*
Gorbachev, Mikhail. *Perestroika*
Hoover, J. Edgar. *Masters of Deceit*
_____. *A Study of Communism*
John Paul II, Pope. *Dominum et Vivificantem* ("On the Holy Spirit in the Life of the Church and the World")
John XXIII, Pope. *Mater et Magistra* ("On Christianity and Social Progress")
_____. *Pacem in Terris* ("Peace on Earth")
Miceli, Vincent P. *The Gods of Atheism*
Payne, Robert. *The Life and Death of Lenin*
Paul VI, Pope. *Ecclesiam Suam* ("On the Church")
Pius XI, Pope. *Divini Redemptoris* ("On Atheistic Communism")
Pius XII, Pope. *Ad Apostolorum Principis* ("On Communism and the Church in China")
Shams, Abdul. *In Cold Blood: The Communist Conquest of Afghanistan*
Shifrin, Avraham. *The First Guidebook to Prisons and Concentration Camps of the Soviet Union*
Shub, David. *Lenin: A Biography*
Solzhenitsyn, Aleksandr. *The Gulag Archipelago*
Valladares, Armando. *Against All Hope*
Vatican II. *Pastoral Constitution on the Church in the Modern World*
Weyl, Nathaniel. *Red Star Over Cuba*
Wolfe, Bertram D. *Three Who Made a Revolution*

Chapter 16

A Movement That Changed the World

Purpose: The purpose of this chapter is to discuss the predictions of the Blessed Mother about the historical advance of communism, the warnings of Pope Pius XI, and the philosophy of the Marxist-Leninists.

Tips for Teachers: First, review with the students the startling predictions of the Blessed Mother at Fatima on July 13, 1917, and show that they have come true. The message of Fatima—prayer, penance, and reparation for sin—needs to be brought to the attention of, and put into practice by, many more people if we are ever to achieve a just peace in the world.

Next, discuss with the class the reason for the success the communists enjoyed for seven decades as they captured more than a score of countries and enslaved over a third of the world's population. Their success had little or nothing to do with the appeal of the Marxist-Leninist philosophy; it was rather because, as Pope Pius XI suggested, too few people were able or willing to grasp the true nature of communism.

It is still important today that we study the principal beliefs of the communists and place them in their historical context so that we can learn from the mistakes of the past in dealing with totalitarians and not repeat those mistakes in the future. Review the communist attitude toward other governments, economics, morality, and private property. The ten points listed in the *Communist Manifesto* are a blueprint for tyranny and should be explained and discussed.

Topics for Discussion:

1. Why did the Blessed Mother feel it necessary to tell the three young shepherd children at Fatima about great world events that were still years in the future?

2. Why did so few people heed the warning of Pope Pius XI in his encyclical on Atheistic Communism?

3. If a Pope today were to ask your advice on what to say in a letter to the world, what would you tell him?

4. What is the most compelling argument against communism?

5. What is dialectical materialism and what is wrong with it?

6. Why did communists give top priority to abolition of private property?

Some Questions and Answers:

1. Are Catholics required to believe in the appearances of the Blessed Mother at Fatima and other places?

A. Belief in these apparitions is not required of Catholics as part of the "deposit of faith" left to us by Jesus, but many are well authenticated and have been approved by the Church. Pope John Paul II, who visited Fatima several times, said on one occasion that "Marian shrines and places of pilgrimage are a kind of 'geography' of faith by which we seek to meet the Mother of God in order to find a strengthening of our Christian life. Popular devotion to the Blessed Virgin Mary is rooted in sound doctrine."

2. Was there ever any indication that the communists intended to bring about a classless society where everyone would be equal?

A. If there ever was such an indication, it was kept well hidden. Marxist-Leninists spouted the theory of the state withering away, but in practice they held on tight to their dictatorial power and their luxurious lifestyle right up until some of them, like Nicolae Ceausescu in Romania, were caught and executed by their former subjects. Under these totalitarian socialists, the people were equal all right—equally poor, equally hungry, and equally subjugated.

3. What was all the controversy about communists in our government back in the 1950s? Wasn't that a lot of nonsense?

A. In point of fact, the Soviet Union was very successful in recruiting Americans to spy against the United States, to steal secret papers and documents, and to influence American policy so that it helped Marxist-Leninists achieve some of their goals. The voluminous record, including recently released files from Soviet archives, shows that Soviet penetration of the U.S. Government began in the 1930s and extended from the lower ranks to top-level policy and operating positions in our government. Hundreds of congressional reports document this communist success, and one book that summarizes it very well is James Burnham's *The Web of Subversion*.

Those willing to betray their own country were still active in the 1980s when a spy ring was uncovered in the U.S. Navy after it had sold to the Soviet Union over a 17-year period a million or more messages and the keys to decipher them. See John Barron's book, *Breaking the Ring*, for the details.

And even in the early 1990s, the FBI was expressing concern about hundreds of Russian agents who were entering the United States disguised as tourists and businessmen but intent on stealing weapons, computers, and communications technology. This was after hostile relations between the United States and Russia were supposed to have ended, and it's one reason why caution is still necessary in any dealings with those who no longer call themselves communists but who still act like communists.

Projects:

1. Read one of the books on Fatima and list for the class the predictions that Mary made about Russia and the remedies that she promised would bring about world peace.
2. Read Pope Pius XI's encyclical on Atheistic Communism and discuss three things that he found bad about communism.
3. Organize a prayer service, featuring the rosary, for all those still living under totalitarianism and for world peace.

References:

Barron, John. *Breaking the Ring: The Bizarre Case of the Walker Family Spy Ring*
Carroll, Warren. *70 Years of the Communist Revolution*
Carson, Clarence. *Basic Communism: Its Rise, Spread and Debacle in the 20th Century*

Chambers, Whittaker. *Witness*
Conquest, Robert. *The Great Terror*
Fox, Robert J. *Fatima Today*
Hoover, J. Edgar. *Masters of Deceit*
_____. *A Study of Communism*
John Paul II, Pope. *Dominum et Vivificantem* ("On the Holy Spirit in the Life of the Church and the World")
John XXIII, Pope. *Mater et Magistra* ("Christianity and Social Progress")
Lyons, Eugene. *Workers' Paradise Lost*
Pelletier, Joseph. *The Sun Danced at Fatima*
Pius XI, Pope. *Divini Redemptoris* ("On Atheistic Communism")
Shams, Abdul. *In Cold Blood: The Communist Conquest of Afghanistan*
Solzhenitsyn, Aleksandr. *The Gulag Archipelago*
Walsh, William Thomas. *Our Lady of Fatima*

Chapter 17

Marxism and Religion

Purpose: The purpose of this chapter is to show that Marxism-Leninism was and always will be a mortal enemy of religion in general and the Catholic Church in particular and that the differences between them cannot be reconciled.

Tips for Teachers: Religion has always been a major obstacle to the spread of totalitarian systems, including Marxism-Leninism, because its loyalty to God conflicts with loyalty to the all-powerful state. Communism demanded complete and total dedication to the state, something which religious people could not give, and so organized atheists stirred up hatred and persecution of all religions, and especially the Catholic Church. The state is the "god" of totalitarians, and they do not permit the worship of any other god.

Catechists must make clear that Marxism-Leninism and Christianity are diametrically opposed to each other, and this hostility can be most clearly demonstrated by the savage communist persecutions of religions and religious leaders, such as those in Russia, Spain, Hungary, Poland, and Cuba. Even Pope John Paul II was not exempt from an assassination effort by the communists in 1981.

This hatred and hostility can also be shown in regard to such issues as the existence of God, the worth of the individual, and the moral law. Stress the communist concept of morality—that whatever advances the cause of Marxism-Leninism is good, and whatever retards that cause is bad—and point out that one must grasp this fundamental tenet of communism if one is to understand why they have acted the way they have. It is very difficult for people with moral standards to conceive of anyone totally devoid of such standards, but such people do exist and they wreaked havoc on the world for most of the twentieth century.

Marxist efforts to undermine the Catholic Church were not always as blatant as the persecution of a Cardinal Mindszenty or the murder of a Father Popieluszko. They were also subtle, such as the use of "liberation theology" in Nicaragua and other Latin American countries. Make sure the class understands why this approach is wrong and dangerous.

Topics for Discussion:

1. Why can't a Catholic be a Marxist or a communist?
2. Why has the Catholic Church always been a prime target of communists and other totalitarians?
3. What is the communist attitude toward morality?
4. What are some of the fundamental points of conflict between Christianity and Marxism-Leninism?

Some Questions and Answers:

1. Persecution of the Catholic Church has produced great heroes and martyrs in every century. Can you name some modern examples?
A. There have been literally thousands, and perhaps hundreds of thousands, of religious people who have heroically defended their faith, and even given their lives, in the face of communist torture and terror in this century. Most of these gallant souls are known only to God, but those who publicly carried their cross in imitation of Christ would include Maryknoll Bishop James E. Walsh, who was a prisoner of the Chinese Communists from 1958 to 1970; Cardinal Stepan Trochta of Czechoslovakia, who was hounded to death by the communists in 1974; Joseph Cardinal Mindszenty of Hungary, whose twenty-five year struggle with the communists included eight years of mental and physical torture and imprisonment; and Fr. Jerzy Popieluszko of Poland, whose courageous struggle against the communists is chronicled in *The Priest and the Policeman.*

There is also the inspiring story of a Chinese priest named Father Hsia, who was sentenced to twenty years at hard labor for the "crime" of being a priest. A Frenchman who served seven years in a slave labor camp in Communist China told of an incident that occurred on Christmas Day in 1961. Father Hsia had asked the Frenchman to watch for the guards while he went down into a ditch in the rice paddies to pray. After a few moments of anxious watching, the Frenchman went over to the ditch to hurry the priest along, and he described what he saw:

> Down in that dried-up ravine, Hsia was saying Mass. For a church he had this vast wilderness in the north of China, and a frozen mound of earth was his altar. For vestments he wore the tattered prison uniform; a chipped enamel drinking mug served as his chalice. Out of a few long-hoarded grapes, he had managed to contrive something resembling wine, and from a handful of wheat which he must have stolen during the summer harvest he had made a thin biscuit to use as the host.
>
> No candles flanked Hsia's altar; in their stead a tiny flame flickered above a few sticks of kindling. For a choir there was that wind out of the northwest that blew on and turned into a hymn, and it seemed to me then that the flames were sending the brave old man's prayers straight up to heaven, while the wind spread them to the four corners of the world.
>
> Suddenly, I yearned to share Hsia's faith. Nowhere in the world on this Christmas Day, I thought, not in the grandest churches of Christendom, could anyone be celebrating a Mass as meaningful as this one. . . . A few days later, there was another cell transfer, and Hsia and I were sent separate ways. I never saw him again. . . . Hsia may be alive today, or he may be dead. But even if the communists have killed him, they have destroyed only the body that housed his unconquerable soul. That will always remain beyond their reach (Jean Pasqualini, "The Christmas Mass of Father Hsia," *Reader's Digest*, January 1970, pp. 143-144).

2. Is it true that some religious leaders actually joined forces with the communists? How could they work with those who were so hostile to God and religion?

A. Some clergymen were duped into supporting communist programs because they thought they were working for peace or racial justice or some other worthwhile goal and didn't realize that they were being manipulated by communists. Others, however, knew exactly what they were doing, like those Catholic priests who joined the communist government in Nicaragua and then publicly defied Pope John Paul II when he told them to sever their ties with the communists during his visit to that country in 1983.

What motivated the priests in Nicaragua, we don't know, but in many cases it was not so much the clergy becoming communists, but rather communists becoming clergy. Some went through the whole process of study and training, and perhaps even years of service in a particular church or institution, before showing their true colors. Many people find it hard to understand such patience and dedication in the cause of evil, but this is another reason why Marxist-Leninists were so successful. If Christians had their zeal, Christianity would have prevailed over communism in many areas of the world instead of the other way around.

Projects:

1. Read one of the references listed below and report to the class.
2. Make a poster showing the contradictions between communism and Christianity.
3. Say the rosary every day that freedom and justice will be spread throughout the world.

References:

Carroll, Warren. *70 Years of the Communist Revolution*
Carson, Clarence. *Basic Communism: Its Rise, Spread and Debacle in the 20th Century*
Ciszek, Walter J. *He Leadeth Me*
_____. *With God in Russia*
Clifford, John W. *In the Presence of My Enemies*
Conquest, Robert. *The Great Terror*
Fox, Robert J. *Fatima Today*
Galter, Albert. *The Red Book of the Persecuted Church*
Hoover, J. Edgar. *Masters of Deceit*
_____. *A Study of Communism*
Kerrison, Raymond. *Bishop Walsh of Maryknoll*
Mindszenty, Jozsef Cardinal. *Memoirs*
Moody, John, and Boyes, Roger. *The Priest and the Policeman*
Pelletier, Joseph. *The Sun Danced at Fatima*
Pius XI, Pope. *Divini Redemptoris* ("On Atheistic Communism")

Sacred Congregation for the Doctrine of the Faith. *Instruction on Certain Aspects of the Theology of Liberation*
_____. *Instruction on Christian Freedom and Liberation*
Solzhenitsyn, Aleksandr. *The Gulag Archipelago*
Sterling, Claire. *The Terror Network*
_____. *The Time of the Assassins*
Valladares, Armando. *Against All Hope*
Walsh, William Thomas. *Our Lady of Fatima*
Wurmbrand, Richard. *Tortured for Christ*

Chapter 18

The Christian Response

Purpose: The purpose of this chapter is to review some effective ways to combat Marxism-Leninism and to bring about the reformation of society with Christian principles.

Tips for Teachers: Refer back to Pope Pius XI's encyclical on Atheistic Communism to see how well he understood the nature of the communists. We must try to create that same understanding today so that the forces of Marxism-Leninism will remain in retreat and future generations will not fall for another version of their diabolical propaganda.

Remind the students of their obligation to expose and fight all forms of totalitarianism, even if it means being ridiculed by others. Any sincere and dedicated follower of Christ should not expect treatment different from what our Lord himself received when he tried to impart religious values and principles to the people of his day.

Stress that communism was never a mystery and that it never tried to conceal its real goals and objectives. Yet a lot of people were taken in by the smiles and double-meaning phrases of leading communists. And even as these words are written and people are saying that communism is dead, there are still millions of our brothers and sisters who are living under totalitarian regimes of the Marxist, communist, or socialist variety.

Catechists must remind the students not to be indifferent to the plight of these millions. We must never cease praying and calling for true freedom and justice throughout the world, recognizing and actively opposing those who would deny people these rights, and promulgating Christian principles as the only alternative to the forces of totalitarianism.

Finally, review with the students the many specific suggestions of what individuals can do and encourage them to put as many of these suggestions into practice as possible. The type of response Christians make today may very well determine the kind of world we will live in tomorrow.

Topics for Discussion:

1. Why are people so unconcerned about organized atheism today?
2. Do you think that lack of concern is justified?
3. What is necessary to help those in countries controlled by dictatorial governments to obtain the same freedoms that we enjoy?
4. What can you do to bring about more awareness of our responsibility to those people?

Some Questions and Answers:

1. What do we need to do to oppose the forces of atheism most effectively?

A. In addition to constant and fervent prayer, especially the rosary, we need to reform our own lives first and become followers of Christ in deed as well as in name. This can never be accomplished unless we lead a healthy spiritual life that includes at least weekly Mass and Communion, frequent Confession, the reading of the Bible and the lives of the saints, and avoidance of sin and the occasions of sin. Once we have reformed our own lives, then we can begin the reform of society and bring about an atmosphere that will prevent ideologies like Marxism-Leninism from ever gaining a significant foothold.

2. How can we be sure that Marxism-Leninism will eventually fail and that Russia and other countries will be completely converted?

A. For one thing, we have the promise at Fatima of the Blessed Mother, who said that Russia will be converted and the world will experience a period of peace if her requests for prayer, penance, and reparation for sin are heeded. And for another, we know that the whole Marxist-Leninist system contains within itself the seeds of its own destruction. In his book *The Gods of Atheism*, Father Vincent Miceli wrote this obituary for Marxism-Leninism:

> It may take a long or short time, but the death of communism is inevitable. A day will come when the forces of de-

cay and revolt within will coincide with the forces of assault and freedom from without; then communism will crumble, be wiped from reality, to be remembered only, like nazism, fascism, and Japanese militarism, as a horrible nightmare that plagued the human race for over half a century.

Father Miceli also reminded us, however, that we must first turn to God and live according to his divine will before communism will be destroyed. He said that "God, who created man without his consent, will not save him without his cooperation, not even from that ultimate spiritual evil, the cancer of communism."

Projects:

1. Learn as much as you can about atheism.
2. Become an active and conscientious citizen and voter.
3. Deepen your spiritual life and your relationship with God.
4. Pray the rosary every day.
5. Organize a public rosary for peace and the complete conversion of Russia.

References:

Carroll, Warren. *70 Years of the Communist Revolution*
Carson, Clarence. *Basic Communism: Its Rise, Spread and Debacle in the 20th Century*
Catechism of the Catholic Church
Fox, Robert J. *Fatima Today*
Hoover, J. Edgar. *Masters of Deceit*
_____. *A Study of Communism*
Miceli, Vincent P. *The Gods of Atheism*
Pelletier, Joseph. *The Sun Danced at Fatima*
Pope Pius XI. *Divini Redemptoris* ("On Atheistic Communism")
Walsh, William Thomas. *Our Lady of Fatima*

Chapter 19

You Can Make a Difference

Purpose: The purpose of this chapter is to show how one person, inspired by Christian love, can truly make a difference in this life.

Tips for Teachers: In the Charles Dickens classic *A Christmas Carol*, there is a scene where Scrooge, having just had a visit from the ghost of Jacob Marley, looks out the window and sees the air full of phantoms and spirits, all of them wandering restlessly, crying and moaning piteously. The reason for their misery, Dickens tells us, is that they had forever lost the power to help others.

In the first chapter, we talked about all the good things that we leave undone, although we still have a chance to make up for it. But suppose, like the spirits in the Dickens tale, we could see all the pain and suffering and tragedy in the world and not be able to lift a finger to help. What a frustrating experience that would be, no longer having the power to do good.

Discuss whether one person really can make a difference and then cite numerous examples of the power of one individual from Church history and American history. Ask the students to come up with examples of their own. We live in an age where doers are needed, not talkers or complainers. We must become instruments of God, as suggested in the prayer of St. Francis. We must become active apostles of Jesus Christ. We must let our light shine forth in a world darkened by sin and selfishness, and then we can say with St. Paul that we have fought the good fight, finished the race, and kept the faith—and now await our reward in heaven.

Topics for Discussion:

1. Can one person really make a difference? Cite some examples.
2. Did God give us a backbone or a wishbone?

3. What are you doing to bring the love and truth of Christ to the world?

4. If you had to choose a time in history in which to live, would you choose today or some other period? Why?

5. If you were arrested as a Christian, would they be able to find enough evidence to convict you of being a follower of Christ?

Some Questions and Answers:

1. What is the prayer of St. Francis?
A. The prayer of St. Francis of Assisi goes like this:

Lord, make me an instrument of your peace. Where there is hatred, let me sow love; where there is injury, pardon; where there is doubt, faith; where there is despair, hope; where there is darkness, light; and where there is sadness, joy.

O Divine Master, grant that I may not so much seek to be consoled as to console; to be understood as to understand; to be loved as to love. For it is in giving that we receive; it is in pardoning that we are pardoned; and it is in dying that we are born to eternal life.

2. Can you mention some modern examples of what one person can do?
A. How about Pope John XXIII, who captured the imagination and love of the world and inspired countless acts of good will during his brief reign as the successor of St. Peter. Or Fr. Patrick Peyton, who carried the Family Rosary Crusade to tens of millions of people in dozens of countries throughout the world. Or Mother Teresa of Calcutta, who started a home for the dying in India several decades ago and whose Missionaries of Charity, working with the poorest of the poor in the slum areas of some of the world's largest cities, have rescued many thousands of derelicts from the gutters and have either nursed them back to health or given them a sense of being loved and wanted before they died.

In American history, did John Paul Jones make a difference when he said that he had not yet begun to fight? Or Nathan

Hale when he said that he regretted having only one life to lose for his country? Or Abraham Lincoln when he freed the slaves and held the Union together during the Civil War? Or American soldiers, sailors, and Marines who fought and died bravely for the freedom of others in the wars of the twentieth century? Or the first astronauts who had the courage to attempt travel into outer space? Or even the ordinary citizens who carry out their daily duties and responsibilities faithfully and cheerfully?

3. What is our greatest need if we are to transform society?

A. Our greatest need is reconciliation with God and with each other, what the Gospel calls an inner renewal that consists of conversion, penance, and a change of heart. Only after we turn inward to God can we then turn outward to society. Only after we get our own spiritual lives in order, primarily through prayer and the sacraments, can we attempt to renew and reform society. True reconciliation with God cannot help but lead to true reconciliation with our neighbor.

Projects:

1. Write an essay on ways that you can make a difference in your immediate family or circle of friends and acquaintances.

2. Read about and report on one of the saints or historical figures mentioned in the chapter.

3. Make the prayer of St. Francis part of your daily prayers.

4. Pray for those working to help others and consider the possibility of a religious vocation, perhaps even in the Missionaries of Charity.

5. Begin your inner renewal today.

References:

Catechism of the Catholic Church
Delaney, John J. *Dictionary of Saints*
Encyclopedia of Church History. Edited by Matthew Bunson
John Paul II, Pope. *Christifideles Laici* ("The Lay Members of Christ's Faithful People")

_____. *Crossing the Threshold of Hope*
_____. *Familiaris Consortio* ("The Role of the Christian Family in the Modern World")
_____. *Redemptoris Missio* ("The Mission of the Redeemer")
_____. *Sollicitudo Rei Socialis* ("On Social Concern")
Vatican II. *Decree on the Apostolate of the Laity*
_____. *Decree on the Church's Missionary Activity*
_____. *Pastoral Constitution on the Church in the Modern World*